DEREK CABRERA & LAURA CABRERA

FLOCK
NOT
CLOCK

DESIGN, ALIGN, *and* LEAD
to ACHIEVE YOUR VISION

**Plectica
Publishing**

Cabrera, D. & Cabrera, L. (2018). *Flock Not Clock: Design,
align, and lead to achieve your vision.* Plectica Publications.
New York.

We would like to thank: our colleagues and our many students at Cornell University who are a great source of insight, joy, passion, and learning; our colleagues around the world who consistently push us to hone our research and share their own; the amazing team at Plectica who have created, and continue to evolve, a remarkable software platform for developing the daily practice of individual and organizational learning; our many clients (many of whom have become good friends) in the profit, nonprofit, and government sectors who have provided us inumerable insights in the implementation of our research, and; our friends and family for their unwavering support.

We'd especially like to thank our parents who did a lot for us, to say the least.

Now that we are parents ourselves, we appreciate them more each day.

FORWARD

Every organization or job that exists today has been influenced in small or large ways by Frederick Winslow Taylor, the father of modern management and organizational theory and the first management consultant. In 1911, his book, "The Principles of Scientific Management" set in motion a century of organizational thinking built on a single paradigm: the modern organization was like a clock. A machine-like collection of people and processes that could be scientifically optimized for control, productivity, efficiency and predictability. Taylor's scientific methods proved efficient, albeit dehumanizing, and were popular in the industrial-factory age. In one iconic example, Taylor increased productivity by over 300% when he designed a new 21lb shovel based on his findings of the average man's optimal shovel load. While Taylor's clockwork approach can still yield productivity gains in highly structured environments (like factories and routinized tasks), today's organizational leaders seeking to create a strong culture of adaptation need a new mindset. They need to think Flock, not Clock.

Adaptive organizations are not like machines. They are more like living organisms. In the same way that individual birds join a flock for collective benefit, this flock mindset enables leaders to harness the power of their people's innate desire to think deeply, create freely, and solve problems. Like all forms of organization, companies are governed by four functions: Vision, Mission, Capacity, and Learning (VMCL). Throughout this book, we will guide you through VMCL using a straightforward check list. By the time you are done, you will have the blueprint to build the culture you need to attain your ultimate goal: to have your entire organization, at every level, working toward realizing your company's vision.

4 FUNCTIONS OF ORGANIZATIONS

Vision (V)	Desired future state or goal
Mission (M)	Repeatable actions that bring about the vision
Capacity (C)	Systems that provide readiness to execute the mission
Learning (L)	Continuous improvement of systems of capacity based on feedback from the external environment

CHAPTER 1 FLOCK NOT CLOCK

FLOCK NOT CLOCK

The best companies know, without a doubt, where the real productivity comes from. … It comes from engaging every single mind in the organization, making everyone part of the action, and allowing everyone to have a voice in the success of the enterprise.

— Jack Welch

Why do we start organizations in the first place? We have a vision for the future, and we need to work with other people to bring that vision to life. We wouldn't start a company to do something we could do on our own, because, let's be honest, working with other people is a pain in the neck. It requires patience and coordination—there are transaction costs. We only start organizations when we can't do what we want to do alone. In short, the whole purpose of any organization is to achieve collective action.

We often find that when an organization is failing to adapt and thrive, it is a result of the failure to harness the power of individuals to drive toward a singular vision. Most of us work hard each day, focused on our goals and daily tasks, meeting and collaborating with other people similarly focused on their own goals and daily tasks. Because our experience of our

work is local, not global, it is easy to lose sight of how this work is connected to the organization's wider vision. Over time, this myopia can be fatal. In most cases, organizational failure doesn't happen quickly. It is the result of a slow leak from work effort that is not connected to the overall vision, a leak of precious resources. For an organization to survive, individuals must work collectively, guided by a shared vision.

In our search for models of how this collective action toward survival is best achieved, we turn to the expert: nature. There are plenty of helpful models to consult: beehives, ant colonies, fish schools, ecosystems, even human networks. Humans are every bit as much a part of nature as any other species. We build big skyscrapers; so do termites. We have sophisticated communications; so do killer whales. Granted, we humans are pretty damned good at a lot of things, but one area in which we could really learn more from the experts is in how to organize ourselves.

Imagine we want to create an intelligent ant colony, but all we have is a bunch of ants with very small brains. What do we do? Let's start an ant training school to make the ants smarter! But the truth is, each individual ant is and always will be limited by its small brain. So how do we "make" them collectively smart? *We give them simple rules.*

Place three piles of food at increasing distances around an ant hill and watch what happens (Figure 1.1). The closest pile gets carried back to the hill first. The second closest goes second. The pile that is farthest away goes third. How are dumb ants all of the sudden acting in intelligent ways that both maximize efficiency and minimize exposure to predation? The answer lies in the simple rules they follow: (1) look for food; (2) if you find food, shoot pheromones out of your butt; and (3) never cross a pheromone trail. These rules, on initial inspection, don't scream intelligence. But intelligence is what emerges out of this banal collective behavior.

What we are seeing in action here is a superorganism—a bunch of independent organisms acting in unison. Superorganisms are remarkable because they transform self-interested, autonomous agents into a powerful, adaptive, self-sustaining, intelligent collectivity. Rather than requiring the constant intervention of leaders, individual agents in a superorganism self-organize by following simple rules that guide their actions in variable contexts.

You want your organization to be more like a superorganism. You want it to adapt quickly to the changing environment, be resilient when times are tough, and be dynamic and alive, because you need it to attract other living things—namely, human talent. Applying nature's secrets about how complex systems work is transformative in today's ever-changing, competitive, complex world. Nothing on the planet beats nature for its resolution of

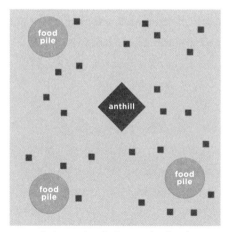

Ants randomly forage for food

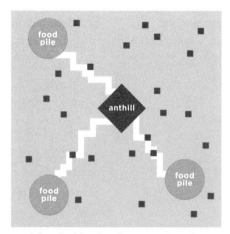

A few find food and communicate by leaving a pheromone trail increasing probability of collective action on food piles

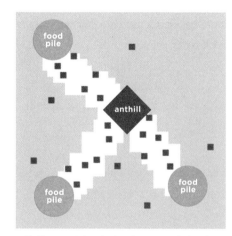

Self-organizing behavior around simple rules produces collective intelligence

Figure 1.1: Smart global behavior is based on simple local rules

paradoxes, elegance of design, and sheer creativity and genius. A key lesson from nature is that your organization is a *complex adaptive system*. The degree to which you lead and manage it as such will largely determine its success or failure.

Complex Adaptive Systems

Take a look at the flocking behavior of what amounts to millions of starlings—a superorganism. Look at how quickly the birds pivot from all moving left to all moving right.

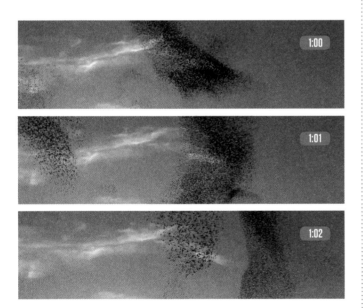

Figure 1.2: A superorganism's adaptive behavior is carried out by agents following simple rules (https://youtu.be/GjwvsK-6640)

How do they do it? These types of systems are evident across the physical, natural, and social sciences in flocks, schools of fish, patterns of traffic, colonies of ants, and across the spectrum of nature and human society–and they baffled scientists for years. It seemed inconceivable that this organized group behavior could occur in the absence of a leader, and yet there is simply not enough time for any communication signal to pass between a leader and the followers. What, then, causes this behavior? It turns out it isn't directed by leaders, but driven by followers. And what are they following? Simple rules.

Iain Couzin,[1] who studies collective animal behavior at Princeton University, did a simulation to show exactly what rules these flocks were following and he found just three:

1. Maintain a constant distance from nearest neighbors.
2. Adjust direction based on nearest neighbors.
3. Avoid predators.

If you watch Figure 1.2 in action, you can actually see the simple rules being followed through the system as predatory hawks attempt to catch the birds. The birds at the bottom of the flock are following rule 1 (constant distance) and rule 2 (adjust direction) and have no idea that rule 3 (avoid predators) was followed above.

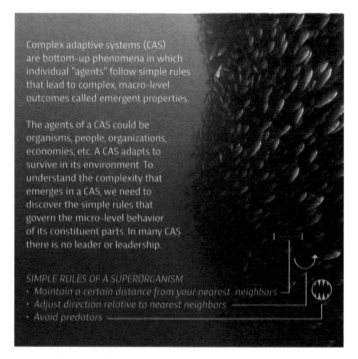

Complex adaptive systems (CAS) are bottom-up phenomena in which individual "agents" follow simple rules that lead to complex, macro-level outcomes called emergent properties.

The agents of a CAS could be organisms, people, organizations, economies, etc. A CAS adapts to survive in its environment. To understand the complexity that emerges in a CAS, we need to discover the simple rules that govern the micro-level behavior of its constituent parts. In many CAS there is no leader or leadership.

SIMPLE RULES OF A SUPERORGANISM
· Maintain a certain distance from your nearest neighbors
· Adjust direction relative to nearest neighbors
· Avoid predators

Figure 1.3: Complex adaptive system (CAS)

Humans do this, too. The largest human wave measured to date consisted of more than 157,000 individuals at a NASCAR race, a planned event to achieve a world record (you can watch it at https://youtu.be/H0K2dvB-7WY). Yet spontaneous waves happen at sporting events all the time, with thousands of individuals acting as a single superorganism, all following one simple rule: do what the person to your left does. When they stand, you stand; when they sit, you sit. There's a relatively simple formula for these complex adaptive

systems: autonomous agents follow simple rules based on what's happening locally (that is, around them), the collective dynamics (simple rules) of which lead to the emergence of the complex, system-level behavior we see. Instead of thinking like a field commander perched on a hill trying to design and control the behavior we want to occur, we need to think like individual soldiers and rely on the collective dynamics of the system to emerge: producing adaptivity, robustness, and so forth.

Figure 1.4: 157,000+ fans set a world record for the largest human wave

Simplicity exists in many places in our everyday lives. The problem is that we distrust it. We don't think of simplicity as a good thing. When we think of someone intelligent, we think of someone who speaks in complicated ways, not someone who keeps things simple. When we face complex organizational problems, we don't think the answer is simple.

And yet, examples of simple rules underlying complexity are all around us. Charles Darwin in *On the Origin of Species*

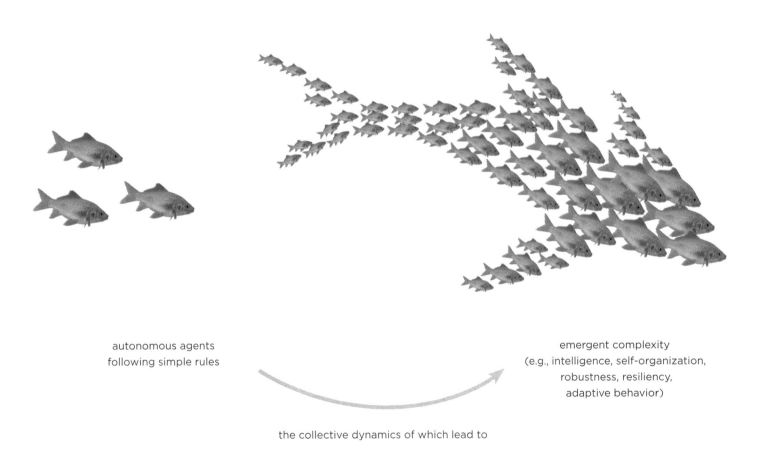

autonomous agents
following simple rules

the collective dynamics of which lead to

emergent complexity
(e.g., intelligence, self-organization,
robustness, resiliency,
adaptive behavior)

Figure 1.5: The basic features of a complex adaptive system

wrote, "from so simple a beginning endless forms most beautiful and most wonderful have been, and are being, evolved."[2] Darwin had only an inkling of what we would later discover to be the hand of DNA—just four base pairs of DNA combine and recombine to create astonishing biodiversity. We can combine just four colors—cyan, magenta, yellow, and black (or CMYK)—to create a full spectrum. The game of chess has rules simple enough for a child to master, yet there are 318 billion possible ways to play the first four moves. The behaviors (or outputs) of systems—be they a flock of starlings or biodiversity writ large, chess matches or organizations—are emergent properties of *simple rules at the local level*. By identifying, understanding, and applying these simple rules, we can make the outputs *better*.

All Organizations Are Complex Adaptive Systems

You don't get to choose whether your organization is a complex adaptive system. All organizations are complex adaptive systems because they are made up of individuals (agents) adapting to their environment. The behavior of an organization—an emergent property of the many agents and their interactions with one another and their environment—is not easily predicted by the behavior of the organizational members alone. As a leader, your challenge is to embrace this reality and leverage it to your advantage.

As complex adaptive systems, all organizations are learning organizations: they test mental models (or schema) of how things work against feedback from the real world. However, in the same way that a child can learn and build maladaptive mental models based on their experience, organizational learning can reinforce maladaptive collective behaviors and cultures. For example:

- A punitive CEO might foster a culture of silence, in which people are afraid to raise concerns or take risks.

- A company that rewards employees for getting along with others and avoiding conflict may never challenge the status quo, thus decreasing creativity and innovation.

- A company built on the successes of a few renegade employees may have difficulty achieving scale.

The ability to adapt is critical for navigating a constantly evolving environment, and cultural norms play an outsized role in determining adaptability. For example, we have worked with a large Chinese conglomerate that was originally a regional airline, an extremely technical and logistics-heavy business. Growing into a multinational company meant adding new and less technical products and services. Their highly structured origin model, which focused on engineering, had created a culture which was slower to adapt and evolve toward these less technical opportunities: individual employees accustomed to being highly directed by leaders and required detailed specifications in order to move forward on a project. The CEO wanted them (and needed them) to have more freedom to operate and adapt in creative ways which would create opportunities for new business segments and new markets.

As complex adaptive systems, all organizations are learning organizations: They test mental models (or schema) of how things work against feedback from the real world.

The ability to adapt is critical for navigating a constantly evolving environment, and cultural norms play an outsized role in determining adaptability. For example, in our work with General Electric (GE), we see a company in the midst of a major adaptation. GE was *the* industrial leader. But when manufacturing went agile and new technology made it possible to 3D print even the most sophisticated parts, the environment shifted relatively quickly from industrial to digital industrial. GE's leadership saw the future and recognized that in order to continue their leadership into that future, they would need to change their existing industrial mental models to digital industrial mental models.

The challenge is to create an organization that learns how to *survive* and *thrive* through adaptation. We need organizational learning that is focused on improving our capacity to achieve our organizational goals. We need systems to ensure that the most productive individual learning is disseminated throughout the organization.

From our understanding of complex adaptive systems, we know that if we want to influence the emergent properties of a system, we need to tweak the agents and/or the simple rules. To create system-level behavior, we must focus on the underlying rules that produce it. Therefore, a leader's power lies principally in selecting agents and deciding, implementing, and enculturating simple rules for the organization.

We want our mental models to align with how the real world actually is. We live a world characterized by volatility, uncertainty, complexity and ambiguity (VUCA). And while the real world is VUCA, we tend to think about the world in linear, anthropocentric, mechanistic, ordered (LAMO) ways. This mismatch has several implications, as you can see in Table 1.1.

VUCA World	LAMO Thinking
The real world is nonlinear...	but, we think in linear ways.
The real world is agnostic about human endeavors...	yet, we tend to look at things through a human-centered (anthropocentric) lens.
The real world is adaptive and organic...	yet, we tend to think mechanistically and the metaphors we use reference machines (e.g., universe is like a clockwork; mind is a computer).
The real world is networked and complex with a sprinkling of randomness...	yet, we think of things in ordered categories and hierarchies.

Table 1.1: VUCA world, LAMO thinking

In short, our thinking is biased in ways that don't align with objective reality. We project this bias onto the world and often miss the critically important feedback the world is giving us—feedback from a multitude of sources. And feedback is critical for fueling our learning, development, and adaptation, as individuals and as organizations. So what is the source of our bias? How do we come to understand it, and how do we change it? In large part, it comes down to mental models.

MENTAL MODELS

Although it feels to our conscious self that we interact directly with the real world, in fact we interact *indirectly* with the real world through our mental models of it. Think of a mental model as a lens between you and reality, coloring what you see.

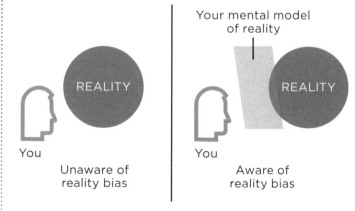

Figure 1.6: Reality bias. The grandfather of all biases

Whether we construct them as individuals or whether we inherit them as part of our culture, we have the power to shift our mental models. But first, we need to recognize that we have them.

Mental models can be simple or wildly complex. They can describe important or unimportant phenomena. Mental models all try to explain or relay some meaning about the nature of our reality. It might be a tiny slice of reality, like how to better cook a scrambled egg, or discovering why a guy at work behaves in such a mean-spirited way or broader, such as why racism persists, or why some people think it doesn't. Our mental models might address how to better construct a democratic society, how to educate our children better, or how to best measure and evaluate our employees.

We humans create mental models that summarize and are capable of describing, predicting, and altering behavior. In other words, our mental models may lead us to think certain things about the real world and result in *actual behaviors* in the real world.

There are many thousands of mental models floating around in an organization with more being floated every day. There are important ones, less important ones, right ones, and wrong ones. Mental models about what kinds of snacks to serve at the snack stations, which processes work best, what

software platform is the best fit, who your customer is… the list goes on and on. But all of these mental models need to "roll up" into a few of the most important mental models for the entire organization. Those mental models need to be shared and, ideally, they shouldn't be chosen arbitrarily, but on the basis of core functions. Your agents (employees) should be armed with these core, functional, "rolled up" mental models as simple rules.

Beware the Four Flawed Mental Models of Organizations

Our more complex problems come about when how we *think* our organization works is out of alignment with how it *actually* works. The traditional model of organizations is based on several significant mental model errors. Why are we committed to a model that is so often wrong? The starting point for these thinking errors is the overarching metaphor that we use to think about organizations: a clock or a machine that can be engineered, tweaked, retooled, recast, or fully understood. Organizations are more organic, adaptive, human, complex, and volatile than clocks. They are not like clocks. The traditional model of organizations can be summarized as plan, command, control, and utilize resources. To say there is room for improvement here is a wild understatement.

Traditional "Clockwork" Leadership

1. Overengineer plans

2. Command hierarchies (org charts)

3. Control processes (flow charts)

4. Utilize a workforce (manage human resources through command and control)

Table 1.2: Traditional model of organization

Flawed Mental Model 1: Plan

First, we need a plan. We used to think we could plan 10 years in advance. Then someone figured out that was crazy talk and the five-year strategic plan was born. Ironically, it took more than five years to realize that five years is also a really long time. Compounding this problem is the fact that the speed of change in markets, society, culture, and technology is accelerating, making each year an even longer time, relatively speaking. So we moved to the two-year plan. The two-year plan was much better because it was nearly 60% more accurate! Of course, we soon realized this, too, was a really long time in business years, which are roughly akin to dog years. So we've settled on "We just need a business plan because we can't get money without one." The basic idea is that there is something magical about a plan. You need to have a plan… or do you?

We are not against planning. We are against hubris. Planning, as it is currently practiced, looks a lot like hubris. Hubris that you can predict the future and account for all the variables and all the actors in the complex system that makes up your business, your market, your industry, or the global economy. The truth is there's a lot of luck and randomness in complex systems. And there's a lot of complexity and interactions that cannot be known. Unless you have a crystal ball (or Google's server data), you're better off focusing on simple rules rather than trying to predict the future.

Not all planning is bad. But we must put planning in real VUCA world contexts to understand their utility. General and later president, Dwight D. Eisenhower, said, "In preparing for battle I have always found that plans are useless, but planning is indispensable." To plan is to think through all the possible alternatives and weigh the pros and cons of each. But we cannot get locked into our plans despite the changing environment, or even confirm their assumptions (confirmation bias) because we are so invested in seeing the outcomes the way we'd planned them. We should keep in mind the saying popularized by John Lennon: "Life is what happens when you are making other plans." So, first and foremost, we must remember that plans are merely mental models about the future and how it will play out, and we must ensure that we update those plans constantly as we get new feedback, information, or signals from the real world.

The second thing to remember about planning is that if planning is a line, made up of some number of points, there are two points on that line that are the most important to clarify with your team: Be brutally honest about where you are—your starting point—and be crystal clear about where you want to go—your ending point or goal. As a long-time mountain guide, I watched confirmation bias and reality bias in action more times than I wish to remember when I watched groups reading maps, orienting themselves to the real world mountain environment, wishing they were standing somewhere they were not and making the terrain fit their mental model of where they thought they were. They didn't trust the terrain, they didn't trust the contour lines of their map, and they didn't trust their compass. They trusted their deep desire not to be in a place that meant they had a long day, a steep climb, or a difficult challenge ahead. Being brutally honest about where you are—when your product isn't up to snuff, when your mental model is flawed, when your customers are disappointed, when you are the problem—is the first and most important point on that planning line. The second is the end point. The vision. Ensuring that everyone has the same goal ensures that at each point each person is attempting to maximize the chances of reaching that goal. We will talk a lot about this ending point in Chapter 2 (Vision).

But if we want to understand how a bunch of people are somehow going to start acting like a superorganism to get things done in an adaptive way, then we need to revisit simple rules and complexity. The best way to get a group of people to work together to bring out the power of their collective dynamics is to give them a simple set of rules and a shared vision (a North Star, so to speak). Think of it this way: if you want a group of people to end up in a particular location, you have to tell them where it is, motivate them intrinsically and extrinsically to get there, and tell them the rules they should follow on the journey. What you don't want to do is micromanage the journey, because things on the ground might be difficult and complex and require adaptivity and grit. What you want to say is: here's the destination in all its glory and here are rules for getting there. So let's say you know where you are and where you want to go (vision). We've been taught since third grade that the shortest path between two points is a straight line. And since third grade we've been imposing this limited truism like a bully on every process we meet. Although it's mathematically true that the shortest path between two points is a straight line, it's not necessarily true in practice when we have countervailing forces and unknown or unexpected variables. Let's say, for example, that in between point A and point B there is a swamp. Add alligators and botulism to the swamp and suddenly the most costly, most time-consuming path is the straight line. Yet this straight line or linear mental model is more popular than you might think. We use it whenever we think that the path between A and B is completely definable even though it is a path in the future through a complex and ever-changing landscape.

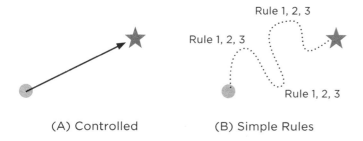

(A) Controlled   (B) Simple Rules

Figure 1.7: Contrasting mental models of process

Figure 1.7 shows two different mental models. In (A) we see where we are, where we want to go, and how we will get there. This represents linear thinking. In (B) we see where we are and where we want to go, but our journey is a bit different. Instead of a simplistic and linear projection, we take into account the unknown. This path is nonlinear, projected rather than definitive, and adaptive, using simple rules to guide what might be a complex trip.

Flawed Mental Model 2: Command

Second, we need a command structure. Everyone loves hierarchical trees, so let's use them. In fact, when you really want to understand an organization and how it works, simply ask to see their organizational chart, or "org chart" (see Figure 1.8). That is the best indicator of how things work in an organization. Because everyone knows that if your boss asks you to do something you definitely do not want to do, or that you disagree with, there is always a way to manipulate or

otherwise obfuscate in a way that effectively means it won't get done.

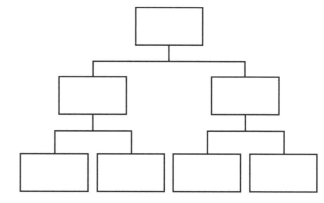

Figure 1.8: Hierarchical org chart

The org chart indicates who is who's boss, who reports to whom, who to see if you have a problem. The truth is it's bunk. It's not how organizations work. Sure, bosses can delegate, hire, and fire, tell employees what to do and, to some degree, use hierarchical power to get them to do it. But it's also true that employees can stall, drag their feet, ignore, play dumb, play dead, or raise Cain. Direct reports can—and more often than not do—make the ultimate decision on what they do. If they have to do something, they can decide to be strategically compliant rather than authentically engaged. They are in charge of how well it gets done. None of that is captured in an org chart. Yet that kind of stuff constitutes 90% of the workweek.

Organizational Chart

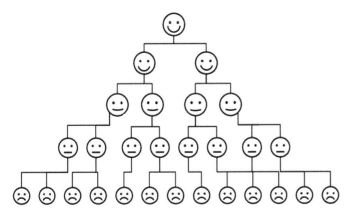

Real Organizational Chart

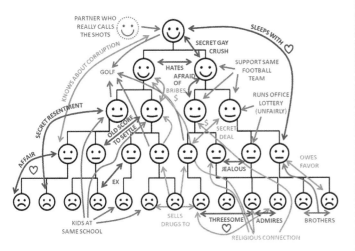

Figure 1.9: Linear mental model versus nonlinear real world

This view of the "real organizational chart" is funny, but in a potentially tragic kind of way. The effects of such a model on an organization can be devastating. When we think of an organization in a simplistic hierarchical way (the mental model on the left) it affects our decisions, behavior, and execution. We believe that things can be done in a top-down (or bottom-up) kind of way. In reality we should be doing things in a networked kind of way, taking into account the influencers and influences that dynamically affect outcomes. When we *think* our organization is a certain way, we behave as if it *is* that way. Worse still, when reality offers us feedback—the lifeblood of survival itself—we misinterpret the feedback because we run it through our mental model of how things are. The effect is that we are a biased buoy at sea, riding the waves in a chaotic fashion, but thinking the waves must certainly have it out for us. We get things wrong, we believe strange things, we become organizational witch doctors.

Why not create a different mental model of an organization—one that better reflects reality? An org chart tells us that our organization looks and acts like a command-and-control hierarchy, when in reality organizations look and act like dynamic social networks (Figure 1.9). In a social network, the nodes (things being connected) are people and the connections (lines) are the relationships between people. The people with the most and highest quality relationships are the most connected, and therefore the most influential in the system. Let's call this the relationship-value (or R-value) of a node. Notably, the thing that we call command and control or hierarchical influence is in actuality the relational influence of the people in the network. So what we should be looking at in our organizations is people and their R-values, or the influence they have on the system.

In healthy organizations, the people with the highest R-values are also the people located near the top of the hierarchy. The stated leaders are the actual leaders. For example, a boss is at the top of the hierarchy because she has more influence, more knowledge, knows more people, has her hands in more processes, and is a part of more initiatives. She's more knowledgeable because she is, and has been, more connected. That's not to say that command-and-control hierarchies don't or can't work. But if you want an adaptive organization, command and control doesn't work. The reason why in the simplest terms has to do with communications and time. Simply put, when something occurs on the ground, the employee needs to respond to it immediately for the organization to be adaptive. In the case of the customer, this is critically important. But if employees have no authority to think or are not incentivized or rewarded for thinking, then they have to go check with higher-ups, sometimes through several levels of command and control. The time it takes for the message to travel up from the employees in the field to the organization's "central nervous system" and then back again kills any hope of a responsive, timely interaction on the ground.

We see this in complex systems in nature. There's simply not enough time to have leaders tell us what to do because leaders can't be everywhere at once. Or can they? What if everyone is given a leadership role in the organization to

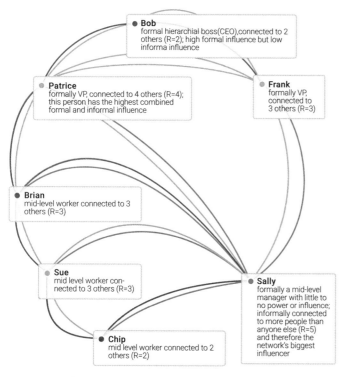

Figure 1.10: Dynamic social network

make decisions locally based on simple rules rather than hierarchical command and control? The org chart mental model versus the social network mental model is important for other reasons. First, the org chart model assumes that people are extrinsically (externally) motivated. What is more likely true is that people are semi-autonomous, somewhat selfish, independent social agents with their own set of extrinsic and intrinsic (internal) motivations. If what the boss is demanding aligns with those motivations, then there is compliance, but if not, the behavior you'll see is false engagement such as strategic compliance, ritual compliance, retreatism, or rebellion.

An employee is strategically compliant when they do what you ask of them for their own strategic interests, which means that as soon as their interests are out of alignment with yours they will not comply. This demonstrates the problem with org charts—they give us the false sense of employee interests being aligned with organizational values. Ritual compliance is when a person complies because they are accustomed to doing so; that is, complies out of habit. That might work for turn-of-the-century factory workers, but not for workers in today's knowledge economies. Today, many jobs require authentic engagement and thinking—even on the assembly line because the tasks, although routine, are highly technical.

Retreatism occurs when a person disengages either physically or mentally, reducing productivity. He shows up and collects a check. Rebellion against the instructions can be either active or passive. Active rebellion is more obvious: for example, storming out of a meeting or refusing to do a task. Passive rebellion is more popular, such as resorting to subversive behavior that can be extremely damaging and costly to your organization. In short, the org chart fails to capture the details of how organizations (and the people who constitute them) actually work. Never before has this been more true than in the current, dramatically changing business climate. Some will argue that command-and-control hierarchies have worked for centuries. And they would be right... sort of. In factory or industrial labor situations, command-and-control hierarchies look like they work because there is more strategic and ritual compliance based on differentials in power and limitations on available choice. But today in market sectors where people shop for workplaces like they shop for the best deals on consumer goods and where hiring the best talent is the crux of organizational success, the best employees have more choices. In addition, in the knowledge age, workers are more educated, more savvy, and more empowered to act upon their own interests. This means that today's org chart mental model is more fiction than fact.

Flawed Mental Model 3: Control

Next (in the traditional model), we need a control structure. We need processes because we need to make sure that we understand every single step of a process that has not happened yet and that will constantly be changing. The ideal structure for this doesn't exist, so we will repurpose our favorite structure of all time: the org chart. Simply turn it on its side and voila—the flow chart. Excellent! An org chart is really just a "tree" network. It follows a pretty typical pattern of branching where there is a trunk (inverted) at the top (CEO) that leads to the main branches (VPs, directors, etc.), which in turn branch down into the next level of hierarchy, and so on.

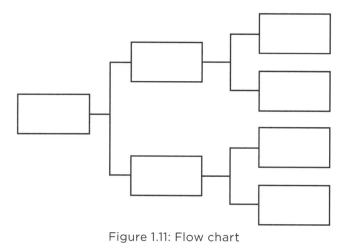

Figure 1.11: Flow chart

We love tree-like charts because we love hierarchies. They make us feel safe. They make us feel like we are in control. They get us. We can't quit them. We love our trees so much that when it comes time to get down to action steps, we head straight for our go-to diagram—the org chart. Org charts make us feel in command of the troops and flow charts make us feel in control of processes. We like to feel in control, even if we are not. Again, we should be clear that org charts or flowcharts are not the enemy. Our concern is with mental models that are out of alignment with reality. Our experience shows that org charts and flowcharts are two of the most popular ways that we incorporate faulty mental models into our organizations. We used a flow chart last week, and not too long ago we used an org chart. The difference was that it was an appropriate use. In the case of the process, it was a very simple, linear process that followed four sequential steps. That's a perfect place for a tree-like flow chart. For simple linear processes, a linear process diagram is a perfectly fine choice.

Flawed Mental Model 4: Utilize

Fourth (in the traditional model), flowcharts, org charts, and plans only work when we have enough human power, so we're going to need some human resources. Also, humans inherently like to think of themselves as resources rather than individuals with their own agency and destiny. That's why they love to join a workforce managed by a Human Resources department. The idea here is to give the humans the plan, give them a flowchart and an org chart, tell them who they report to, and then squeeze the human juice out of them to fuel the machine. It's all very mechanical, but it works, right? Yes. It works. This traditional model of organizations does exactly what it is supposed to do, exactly what it was designed to do: to make us feel in command and in control. It makes little difference to us whether this model of organizations is an accurate reflection of how organizations actually work.

What's important is that it also *feels* like it's working. This warm and fuzzy feeling of control is all we need, until we are faced with results we don't expect. It's these lackluster results that cause us to look for a different model. Ideally, that's when organizations realize their need of systems thinking. Humans are quirky animals. We are independent and seek to differentiate ourselves and our identity and yet we are also extremely social animals who long to be part of a group. We have these amazing logical and analytical abilities (executive functions) and at the same time we can be petty, emotional, and retributive. We are both selfish and social. Businesses of all kinds need resources: financial, physical, and human. We don't think of ourselves as resources. So it's a bit of a disconnect when organizations think of us this way. We have families, loved ones, personal goals, and aspirations. When these priorities, goals, and aspirations align with those of an organization, then it's a great fit. When they don't, it's a bad fit.

Yet the primary mechanism for working with humans is a department we almost always call Human Resources. That's never a good department. We should get rid of that title in exchange for Human Engagement or Human Talent or really anything else that demonstrates an understanding of the paradox that is humanity. People want to improve. They want to be challenged to be better versions of themselves. They want to use their talents to make things better for themselves (selfish) and others (social). We humans like to be engaged in what we are doing. The best way to engage a human is to engage their thinking. Everything else is just strategic compliance. And as soon as the transactional exchange ends, the engagement ends.

But engage people's thinking and you engage their human spirit. You won't get 40-hours a week employees, you'll get employees who think about things in the shower, on the way to work, and before they fall asleep. Extrinsic rewards and incentives (e.g., "carrots") work because we are behavioral animals. We are like Pavlov's dogs. But intrinsic motivation is rooted in engagement. Engagement is the result of three things: using your brain to solve problems, feeling like you're part of something larger than yourself, and affecting change. The greatest threat to the traditional mental model of organizations is results. When we don't get the results we want, we are forced to choose: Do I want to feel in control or do I want to get results? Table 1.3 summarizes the mental models that influence traditional versus systems thinking leadership of organizations.

Mental Model	Traditional Problem	Systems Thinking Solution
Plan	Reality is changing too fast to plan too far out; planning makes us feel like we are in control when we are not; planning introduces biases that can occlude opportunities that arise	Not all planning is "bad"; planning that takes the brutally honest, real-world present situation into account, proposes a future vision of how things can be different, but does not go so far as to outline all the specific steps or paths that must be taken in between those two points can be quite effective
Command	Assuming that your organization is a hierarchical org chart can introduce biases that turn out not to be true; even when hierarchical control does truly exist, it is tempered by social influence, strategic compliance, rebellion, leaks, resistance, and other social phenomena	You are not in command. You (and others) may have disproportionate influence, but no one is in command of a complex system. Thinking of your organization as a complex network that has some hierarchical properties is far more in alignment with reality. Assuming that a command may or may not trickle down and that there are numerous nonhierarchical things that must be done to create cultural change is a far safer bet
Control	We love to feel like we are in control but lackluster results sometimes make us face the reality that we are not; the control paradigm introduces all kinds of cognitive biases that cause us to miss what is really going on	You are not in control (control, no; influence, yes); identifying the points in the system where the right kind of influence can have the right kind of leverage and bring about the desired effect is much more realistic
Utilize	The assumption that people will put up with being used for very long is an unsustainable assumption; even the utilization of resources is a flawed form of thinking that leads to unsustainable practices	People are independent agents in the system; they desire co-evolution where they feel like the goals of the organization and their own individual goals are in alignment; treating people like usable human resources is not going to play out well in reality

Table 1.3: Systems thinking provides new solutions

Vision, Mission, Capacity, Learning

So what are the simple rules of an organization? How do we leverage them to maximize organizational learning, adaptation, and success? These are precisely the questions we have been focused on answering, in our academic research and in our work with corporations. We strive to discover the tools and technology they need to help them adapt and thrive. We have defined four simple, deeply interconnected rules that apply in all types of organizations.

1. Vision (V): The future you see. This is NOT your grandma's vision statement. In Chapter 2, you'll learn that defining your vision—your desired future state—is precise, demanding, and ultimately rewarding work. We will show you how to align all aspects of your organization to bring about this future, so your vision needs to be motivating, simple, and measurable.

2. Mission (M): The actions you take, repeatedly, to bring about your vision. In Chapter 3, we'll make sure you are not putting together a hackneyed hodgepodge of biz speak. Your mission statements will be clear, concise, and measurable.

3. Capacity (C): The systems that provide readiness to execute mission. We will examine how to measure the organizational capacity required to execute your vision day in and day out.

4. Learning (L): Continuous modification of mental models based on feedback from the external environment.

Your vision, mission, capacity, and learning (VMCL) should form the tenets of your culture—they are the key mental models to inculcate. Just as all organizations possess culture, they also possess these natural VMCL functions. Every organization has some ultimate purpose, a desired future state or goal (vision), whether or not it is articulated clearly or widely shared. Similarly, every organization possesses a mission—it takes repeated actions to achieve the vision. All organizations have capacity (adequate or not, ultimately aligned with the vision via the repeated steps of the mission or not). Finally, all organizations (that are complex adaptive systems) learn. That learning may or may not further the vision and increase the organization's fitness.

Simple rule	Short definition
Vision (V)	Desired future state or goal
Mission (M)	Repeatable actions that bring about the vision
Capacity (C)	Systems that provide readiness to execute the mission
Learning (L)	Continuous improvement of systems of capacity based on feedback from the external environment

Table 1.4: VMCL: the simple rules for the CAS that is your organization

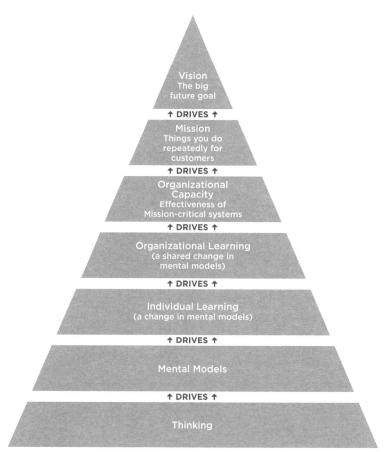

Figure 1.12: Thinking drives Individual and Organizational Learning, which drives Capacity, which drives Mission, which brings about Vision

VMCL is a systems leadership model that helps us to better design, guide, manage, and change our organizations. Throughout this book, we will guide you through VMCL, using the following 20 point check list. By the time you are done, you will have the blueprint to build the culture you need to attain your ultimate goal: to have your entire organization, at every level, working toward realizing your company's vision—your desired future state.

CHECK 1	Our vision depicts a desired future state
CHECK 2	Our vision is intrinsically motivating
CHECK 3	Our vision is short and simple
CHECK 4	We measure our vision
CHECK 5	We ensure our vision lives in hearts and minds
CHECK 6	Our mission is action(s) done repeatedly
CHECK 7	Our mission brings about our vision
CHECK 8	Our mission explains WHO does WHAT for WHOM
CHECK 9	Our mission is clear, concise, and easily understood
CHECK 10	We measure our mission
CHECK 11	We ensure our mission lives in hearts and minds
CHECK 12	We ensure that mission moments are sacrosanct
CHECK 13	We build capacity in order to do our mission
CHECK 14	We build capacity through a system of systems
CHECK 15	We map capacity to understand and better design systems
CHECK 16	We use learning to expand our capacity
CHECK 17	We harness the power of mental models
CHECK 18	We train people to think in order to learn
CHECK 19	We constantly evolve our mental models
CHECK 20	We create a culture of vision, mission, capacity, and learning

CHAPTER 2 SEE VISION (V)

CHECK	1	**Our vision depicts a desired future state**
CHECK	2	**Our vision is intrinsically motivating**
CHECK	3	**Our vision is short and simple**
CHECK	4	**We measure our vision**
CHECK	5	**We ensure our vision lives in hearts and minds**
CHECK	6	Our mission is action(s) done repeatedly
CHECK	7	Our mission brings about our vision
CHECK	8	Our mission explains WHO does WHAT for WHOM
CHECK	9	Our mission is clear, concise, and easily understood
CHECK	10	We measure our mission
CHECK	11	We ensure our mission lives in hearts and minds
CHECK	12	We ensure that mission moments are sacrosanct
CHECK	13	We build capacity in order to do our mission
CHECK	14	We build capacity through a system of systems
CHECK	15	We map capacity to understand and better design systems
CHECK	16	We use learning to expand our capacity
CHECK	17	We harness the power of mental models
CHECK	18	We train people to think in order to learn
CHECK	19	We constantly evolve our mental models
CHECK	20	We create a culture of vision, mission, capacity, and learning

SEE VISION (V)

It is not enough to be industrious; so are the ants.
What are you industrious about?
— Henry David Thoreau

If you want to build a ship, don't herd people
together to collect wood and don't assign them
tasks and work, but rather teach them to long for
the endless immensity of the sea.
— Antoine de Saint-Exupery

Vision is the future you see. Visionary leadership hinges on seeing a future that others can't imagine, standing in that future, and describing what you see. You need to ensure that your organization's resources are aligned with the goal of bringing about this desired future state. We'll get into the how of that in subsequent chapters. But for now, your job as a leader is to craft a vision statement precisely, so that the vision can be readily understood, digested, and internalized. By the end of this chapter, you will understand the benefits of a clear organizational vision, be armed with the structure to articulate yours, and be inspired to do the heavy lifting of enculturating it within your team.

Why Do I Need a Vision?

Given that so many companies lack a vision statement and those that exist exhibit a bizarre range of forms and purposes, you may wonder why you need one. To answer this question, we need to call on what we learned in Chapter 1. Remember that all organizations are complex adaptive systems: they are made up of individual people always interacting with and adapting to their environment. The behavior of an organization (and the attendant outcomes of longevity, profit, growth, reputation, and so forth) is an emergent property of these individuals' interactions with other organizational members and features of the organizational and external environment. This means we can't readily predict organizational outcomes based on group member behavior alone. As a leader, you get to decide whether to embrace the complexity of your organization and leverage it to your advantage through the creation and reinforcement of simple rules and the careful selection of your agents.

What does this have to do with a vision statement? The vision (a desired future goal or state) is a simple rule that must govern the interaction of everyone in the organization. In other words, everything that everyone at every level of your company does should be aligned toward this common goal. Peter Bregman, describing strategy as a people problem, put it best: "To deliver stellar results, people need to be hyper-aligned and laser-focused on the highest impact actions that will drive the organization's most important out-comes. But even in well-run, stable organizations, people are misaligned, too broadly focused, and working at cross-pur-poses."[1] Even a quick mental appraisal of the organizations you belong to—and very possibly your own work patterns—should suggest the difficulty of complete alignment. Certain-ly without a clear, shared understanding of the company's ultimate objective, its *raison d'être*, its North Star, the situa-tion is hopeless.

Figure 2.1: The visionless organization

Indeed, the argument for having an organizational vision is not just conceptual. A study by LRN, a company focused on principles and ethics, found that companies in which employees were primarily motivated by shared values and a commitment to a mission and purpose are nine times more likely to have high customer satisfaction."[2] Although we need more empirical studies of the effects of corporate visions, there is widespread agreement among CEOs about the importance and benefits of defining an organizational vision (though vision is often used interchangeably with mission terminology, which explains the greater prevalence of mission statements).[3] More leaders today appreciate the position of Kevin Plank, founder and CEO of Under Armour, who calls vision his "most important job." [4]

One quantitative longitudinal study that analyzed company financial performance from 2004-2009 found that vision directly affected companies by increasing their sales, employ-ment, and profit. However, the impact of *communicating* cor-porate vision to employees was an even greater determinant of growth in these areas.[5] And a recent Gallup study of vision in almost 200 organizations in 49 industries in 34 countries found a link between profit and vision. The authors wrote, "As employees move beyond the basics of employee engagement and view their contribution to the organization more broadly, they are more likely to stay, take proactive steps to create a safe environment, have higher productivity, and connect with customers to the benefit of the organization."[6]

Beyond these positive associations between articulating a vision and organizational success, there is increasing data suggesting the harm associated with a lack of vision. Gallup's 2017 *State of the American Workplace* report, highlights accelerating changes affecting the workplace. They warn, "The truth is, organizations have nowhere to hide. They have to adapt to the needs of the modern workforce. If they don't, they'll struggle to attract and keep great employees and, therefore, customers." The survey data depict a paucity of faith in leadership. The data are damning: Just 22% of employees strongly agree that leadership "has a clear direction for the organization," 15% strongly agree that leadership makes them "enthusiastic about the future," and only 13% strongly agree that leadership "communicates effectively with the rest of the organization." A key take-away from the report was the urgent need for leaders to "define and convey their vision more clearly and to rally their employees around it."[7]

There is another area in which the data are clear: Most employees are insufficiently aware of and affected by their organization's vision statement. A recent survey found that 58% of employees in a large global sample didn't know their company's vision.[8] Gallup conducted research in 2013 that found leaders, though skilled at process improvements, have a long way to go in terms of sharing core organizational mental models. The associated report explains that many executives don't realize the significance of vision as an asset to improve "organizational performance and profitability, and they neglect their ultimate responsibility of aligning their brand and culture with their highest purpose."[9] The authors identify failure to deal with organizational needs related to vision as a failure of leadership. James Kouzes and Barry Posner, creators of The Leadership Practices Inventory, analyzed the responses of more than one million leaders on the subject of vision, and found that leaders frequently struggle to communicate "an image of the future that draws others in—that speaks to what others see and feel." Yet their research also indicates that this attribute is what most distinguishes true leaders from those who are not leaders.[10]

All of this data suggest two issues we must address: (1) leaders must craft a vision in such a way that it is memorable and influential for employees; and (2) leaders must tirelessly inculcate the vision to the organization.

A Crisis of Disengagement

The Energy Project reports that, as of 2014, "More than 200 studies have now confirmed a direct and powerful relationship between the level of employee engagement and company performance."[11] A worldwide Gallup poll that tracked levels of employee engagement reported that the disengaged employees outnumbered engaged employees by about 2 to 1.[12]

Employee Engagement 2011-2012

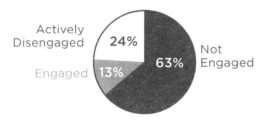

Actively Disengaged / **24%**

Engaged **13%**   **63%**   Not Engaged

In 2014, *The Quality of Life @ Work* survey reported on whether employees are getting their core needs met. [13]

Quality of Life at Work 2014

55%   **54%**

Employees that do not have a "level of meaning and significance" at work

Employees that lack a connection to their company's vision

Employees who found meaning in their work reported being 2.8 times more likely to stay with their company, were 2.2 times more satisfied with their jobs, and 93% more engaged.

The authors concluded, "No single factor in the study influences people's job satisfaction and likelihood to stay at an organization as much as… finding a sense of meaning and purpose in their work."[14]

The data on the consequences of employee engagement speak for themselves, with engaged employees 50% more productive, 33% more profitable, responsible for 56% higher customer loyalty scores, and associated with 44% higher retention rates.[15] These factors in combination produce significant long-term gains.

Without survey data, leaders might equate engagement with behavioral conformity and compliance to norms. In reality, of course, not all engagement is authentic. Folks can be "engaged" in a lot of ways. Remember, you are dealing with a complex adaptive system (CAS); people are semi-autonomous beings with a mix of selfish, other-oriented, and social motivations. They want to belong to groups or seek social approval and therefore follow group norms, including those in the workplace. They also want to be part of something larger than themselves. They both do and don't mind being told what to do, depending on the circumstances. If what the boss is asking of them aligns with their own motivations and goals, authentic engagement is likely. And this applies not just to being asked to do something by a boss but also things they must do in order to be part of the system. (Think of a

CAS in nature: The individual birds engage in the murmurating flock because there is a survival advantage for them.) But if there is not alignment of interests, the behavior you'll see may take many forms of false engagement, such as strategic compliance, ritual compliance, retreatism, or rebellion.

Employees are strategically compliant when they comply solely for their own strategic reasons. As soon as the organization's demands are misaligned with their interests, compliance is unlikely.[16] Ritual compliance—when a person complies because they are accustomed to doing so—is also not a sound basis for any organization in today's knowledge economy. And in today's digital industrial companies, even many factory jobs require people to think and be adaptive. Within the spectrum of engagement is rebellion, which can be either active or overt, but passive rebellion is the most popular form; its characteristic subversive activities and attitudes can deeply undermine your organization. Finally, retreatism (active disengagement) produces untold costs from outright inactivity or marginal productivity.

VISION GIVES US SHARED PURPOSE

Social scientists have long understood the importance humans attach to a sense of purpose and meaning in our lives. Emile Durkheim argued that being bonded to a group with a *shared purpose* is what attaches people to life, and "the lofty goal they envisage prevents their feeling personal troubles so deeply" (as cited in Hechter & Horne, 2009, p.233).[17] Friedrich Nietzsche expresses this another way: "He who has a *why?* to live for can bear almost any *how.*"[18] Most people spend a large portion of their life at work in an organization, and psychologists, sociologists, and social work and management scholars are increasingly aware that the workplace is not and cannot be treated as distinct from other parts of our lives.

In fact, related insights into the importance of motivation in the workplace date back to the management theorists associated with the Human Relations Approach in the 1920s, which envisioned a new role for management that included concern for workers' needs and well-being. Mary Parker Follett, for example, addressed the importance of human relations at work and how individuals relate to the world through their roles as group members. Elton Mayo also emphasized our strong needs for affiliation and paid particular attention to work morale and nonfinancial incentives to increase productivity. The widely read work of Abraham Maslow on the hierarchy of needs was also influential in moving management toward an understanding of the importance of human motivation and personal development.[19]

In the book *Man's Search for Meaning*, Victor Frankl explains that even things that we think of as supremely motivating, like happiness and pleasure, are less motivating than meaning.[20] Daniel Pink in his book *Drive* explains that a sense of autonomy and purpose far outweighs extrinsic incentives.[21] As humans, we crave meaning. A Gallup poll reveals that 83% of people deem it "very important" to believe that their life is meaningful or has a purpose.[22] Given the amount of time we spend at work, the easiest and most logical place for people to meet their needs for meaning and purpose would be on the job. Sadly, that is anything but the case for most of us.

In their book *The Progress Principle*, Harvard Business School professor Teresa Amabile and psychologist Steven Kramer discuss the results of their research into the importance of meaning at work. In their review of daily journal entries, they found that employees who find meaning in their work have a sense of ownership and personal investment. This in turn increases their commitment, intrinsic motivation for and engagement in work—all of which translate into increased productivity and improved performance.[23] A sense of purpose and meaning, a future direction and goal—this is where vision comes in. Before we explain how to create an optimal vision for your company, we need to provide some context on how vision is popularly "understood."

THE SAD STATE OF VISION TODAY

Many companies do in fact articulate a vision, though it often masquerades under different names like purpose or objective, and most frequently as *mission*. As Collins and Porras wrote in 1991, "Most organizations respond to the need for vision by creating something they typically call a 'mission statement.'"[24] Mixing up vision and mission is basically an epidemic among leaders.[25] *This should not be dismissed as semantics*. Vision, mission, capacity, and learning are all natural organizational functions. Vision is the future you see. Mission is the action you take to get there. They are quite different but vitally connected. Much more on that later. For now, let's first provide some context about organizational visions.

Figure 2.2: This Vision Is...Sad

We've taken to snapping photos of visions and missions whenever we see them. This one, from a bank that will remain unnamed to protect the incompetent, made us laugh, but also cry. It was clear that the team that carefully crafted and lovingly printed this vision and mission on foam core didn't have a good idea of the difference between vision and mission or even of what either was. Their vision—"To be the Trusted Resource"—is doubly unmeasurable as both "being" and "trustedness" are ongoing endeavors (a.k.a., moving targets). Worse than that, they've apparently achieved their vision already since their mission states they are the "trusted financial resource." They've arrived! Time to close up shop! This kind of conflation, confusion, and lack of clarity in the flagship mental models of an organization (vision and mission) only amplifies problems downstream. It's no simple thing to find a definition for vision, especially if you're looking for something clear and succinct (say, a single sentence). Often authors will write an entire article about vision without providing a definition. Instead, they will write three paragraphs about what a vision is or is not and how it should function and what benefits it brings. *Business Dictionary* online does not define vision, but does provide one for vision statement: "An aspirational description of what an organization would like to achieve or accomplish in the mid-term or long-term future. It is intended to serves as a clear guide for choosing current and future courses of action."[26] The classic article on vision by Collins and Porras defines vision as consisting of "core ideology" (consisting of core purpose and core values) and "envisioned future" (consisting of big, hairy, audacious goal and vivid description).[27] Still other authors use vision as an umbrella term to incorporate things like mission, values, and strategy.[28]

Conflation, confusion, and lack of clarity in the flagship mental models of an organization (vision and mission) only amplifies problems downstream.

Perhaps the most troubling phenomenon with respect to organizational visions is the mismatch between the importance attributed to them[29] and the fact that so many companies do not articulate one. Even given the tendency to confuse mission and vision (and most companies do have a mission statement), it is dismaying that many organizations do not articulate a desired goal or future state. How can you craft a strategy without an end in mind?

Fortune 500 companies, as an example, demonstrate substantial inconsistency and confusion about vision statements. One study found that fewer than 31% clearly identified a vision, and those that did demonstrated extreme inconsistency in their content and purpose.[30] While authors and consultants use different definitions of vision, there is some consensus around the idea that a vision must be forward-looking and aspirational, yet sufficiently clear to be understood and provide direction.

There is, however, not much consensus on how far into the future a vision should stretch: Coca-Cola[31] and Caterpillar[32] both explain their "2020 vision," while Volkswagen's equivalent to a vision was crafted in 2014 and expires in 2018.[33] Some consultants advise setting your vision for five or 10 years[34] while others advise "medium-term targets,"[35] and still others advise big, hairy, audacious goals (BHAG) which tend to be ambitious and long-term.[36] This noteworthy discrepancy concerning projecting into the future aside, here's a common understanding of vision: "Vision statements are future-based and are meant to inspire and give direction to the employees of the company, rather than to customers."[37]

The following companies' vision statements illustrate the nature of our vision problem. Some are vague (and vapid), while others fail to depict a future state or goal. Others fall short in the inspiration department.

Harley Davidson	"To fulfill dreams through the experiences of motorcycling"
Hilton	"To fill the earth with the light and warmth of hospitality"
Tyson Foods	"Making Great Food. Making a Difference"
Honda	"To Be a Company that Our Shareholders, Customers and Societ Want"
Kraft Foods	"To make today delicious"
Macy's	"Macy's, Inc. is a premier national omnichannel retailer with iconic brands that serve customers through outstanding stores and dynamic online sites"
Boeing	"People working together as a global enterprise for aerospace industry leadership"

Figure 2.3: A sample of vision statements

On the whole, we've become accustomed to vision statements being throw-away lines devoid of meaning and any practical import whatsoever. The opportunity cost of such vague vision statements—or worse, not having one at all—is immense.

CRAFTING A GREAT VISION

In fact, most corporate statements we've encountered—be they called mission, vision, purpose, philosophy, credo, or the company way—are of little value. They don't have the intended effect. They don't grab people in the gut and motivate them to work toward a common end. They don't focus attention. They don't galvanize people to put forth their best efforts toward a compelling goal. They don't mean something to people all up and down the organization. In fact, they are usually nothing more than a boring stream of words.
— Jim Collins and Jerry Porras [38]

Let's build upon our simplest definition of vision—a desired future goal or state. What else must visions be? Well, they must be intrinsically motivating, short, simple, and measurable. *And, they must be enculturated.* We will address these requisite qualities—explaining their importance for your vision—each in turn. Before that, though, two reminders.

1) Vision (like mission, capacity, and learning) is a natural function of any organization, whether or not it is consciously designed and articulated. [39]

2) Vision (like mission, capacity, and learning) is a core tenet of your culture. As such, you need to build and inculcate shared mental models of your vision throughout your organization.

Let's go through five checks for creating a solid vision.

Check #1: Our Vision Depicts a Desired Future State

This is the first checkpoint because we see it as inviolable. If you are going to create a vision for your organization and you do not use it to indicate where the organization is headed, what goal you are aiming for, the desired future state you envision… stop. Don't do it. If you are thinking of describing what your organization does in the present… don't. (Hint: That's your mission.) How can we remember that, above all, the vision must guide us, must allow us to see where we want to go? The noun *vision* has many meanings. All of them suggest the cardinal rule for setting your organization's vision.

- the act or power of sensing with the eyes; sight

- the act or power of anticipating that which will or may come to be: prophetic vision; the vision of an entrepreneur

- an experience in which a personage, thing, or event appears vividly or credibly to the mind, although not actually present, often under the influence of a divine or other agency: a heavenly messenger appearing in a vision[40]

Visionary leadership means seeing a future that others can't envision, standing in that future, and describing what you see. Visions are visual depictions of the place we are going: the proverbial promised land. Leaders must spend time building these vivid images of the future they see, and how it differs from the undesirable and perhaps intolerable present. Differentiating these two pictures is every bit as important as differentiating one's products in the marketplace. It's a compare and contrast exercise: here's a picture of one place, here's one of another. Which one do you like? Okay, B? Well, I can show you how to get there. Thus, a visionary leader is born.

We can't emphasize this enough: Visions exist in the future,[41] not in the present or the past. We often get clients started in the process by asking them what they most want to change about how things are today. We start with people by drawing a line down the center of the board with the present picture of how things are and a future picture of how things should be, as in Activity 2.1.

What do you see today?

Example: An internet based on information

Your turn:

What should we see tomorrow?

Example: An internet based on knowledge

Your turn:

Activity 2.1: Find your vision by contrasting present and future conditions.

An example of a vision that vividly depicted the undesirable present comes from Sony. In the 1950s, their vision was "Become the company most known for changing the worldwide poor-quality image of Japanese products."[42]

Check #2: Our Vision Is Intrinsically Motivating

Like an old-fashioned alarm clock coupled with a hot cup of freshly brewed coffee, your organization's vision should be the thing that gets you going each day. And on the mornings when you don't want to get up, it's the vision that motivates you to drag your sorry ass out of bed and get to work. That's the power of a great vision—it's intrinsically motivating. There are countless opportunities to effectively employ extrinsic rewards in your organization, but the one thing that must be intrinsically motivating is your vision. In sessions with teams when we work on vision development, people get goosebumps when they finally see their vision for the first time. People should be jazzed about it. If they're not, then your vision needs some work.

> There are countless opportunities to effectively employ extrinsic rewards in your organization, but the one thing that must be intrinsically motivating is your vision.

This is why one of the best ways to find your vision is to ask yourself, "What pisses me off?" Or alternatively, "What breaks my heart?" We always say that your vision is something that inspires. In many cases this is because it's the opposite of what drives you crazy, deeply angers you, or causes you sadness. Try this:

What do you see today that pisses you off or breaks your heart?

Example: Presentation software designed for the presenter rather than the audience

Your turn:

What should we see tomorrow that motivates you to work hard to be the catalyst for the change you want to see?

Example: Presentation software designed to make presentations easy to do and enjoyable to experience

Your turn:

Activity 2.2: Visions are often born of things that upset you

It's not uncommon to see a vision statement that reads "To become the top purveyor of widgets across the globe" or whatever industry equivalent makes sense. These are boring and unimaginative. Yes, every business would like to lead the pack. But is that itself a source of deep inspiration on a daily basis? *Fast Company* writer Jessica Amortegui provides guidance on the derivation of purpose at work.

> Consider one computer manufacturer's mission statement: "To be the most successful computer company in the world." That's great. But it displays a major meaning trap that many of us fall prey to–it's all about us. What if the mission statement read: "To be the most successful computer company for the world"? Meaning comes when we realize the impact of our work on others. In fact, what distinguishes the most successful givers–versus those who burnout–is not what or how much they give. It is that they know the difference they make on others. People aren't inspired solely by what they do. People are lit up when they know why what they do matters.[43]

But bear in mind the significance of the vision for everyone in your organization. Everyone needs purpose and meaning in their lives and their work. Let's quantify this a bit for emphasis. Joseph Folkman, noted business author and founder of two leadership firms, writes about how to ensure your vision is valued in your organization.

> Employees who don't find their company's vision meaningful at all have average engagement scores of only 16 percent. These are employees who do not care about the future success of the organization. They work primarily for a paycheck and are willing to do very little beyond what is absolutely required to keep their jobs. Those who find their organizations' vision meaningful have engagement levels that are 18 percentile points above average.[44]

Okay, enough reading. It's time for a quiz.[45]

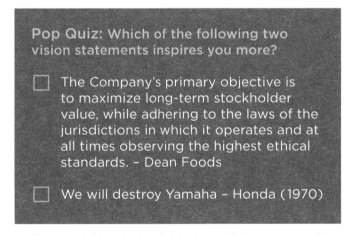

Figure 2.4: How to tap intrinsic motivation: pop quiz

Case: "Living Healthy Is the New Normal"

Let's take a look at a well-built vision created by the folks at MyFitnessPal (MFP). The story of MFP is a fascinating one. Brothers Albert and Mike Lee programmed a "diet app" to lose a few pounds in anticipation of Mike's wedding. They made the app available for free in 2005 and within 10 years the app had 165 million users and they sold MFP to Under Armour for $475 million. But early on in the company's life Mike and Albert realized that MFP's 50+ million active users had (if somewhat unintentionally) become the largest health, nutrition, and fitness dataset in the world. They also realized that these data could be used not only to help individual users make better health decisions through the MFP app, but also to create healthier environments for those individuals to live in everyday. It pissed them off that large portion sizes, constant access to unhealthy foods, and confusing and conflicting health information made it easy to live an unhealthy lifestyle. Put another way, it was difficult to live healthy. The brothers realized that their dataset could influence restaurants and gyms, and social programs and policies in ways that could usher in their global vision: Living Healthy Is the New Normal.

MFP could have chosen "The Best Diet and Fitness App in the Known Universe" as their vision. But, for Albert, Mike, and their team, their goal and source of motivation transcended improving their own lot in life. It was about changing the world. They developed what we call a case for existence: establish an argument (case) for why something should exist and for what purpose. In a case for existence, you or your company become the causal agent that brings about the change from the present

MFP is the causal agent of a different future...
This relationship between present state and future state is altered by MFP. It is our "case for existence"

Today, we live in a state of unhealthy inertia
This present state is what pisses us off about how things are...it contains the passion and impetus for envisioning a new reality

In the future, we envision a world where there is a healthy inertia.
This future state is the basis for our vision: Healthy is the New Normal

Figure 2.5: Original compressed map of MFP vision session

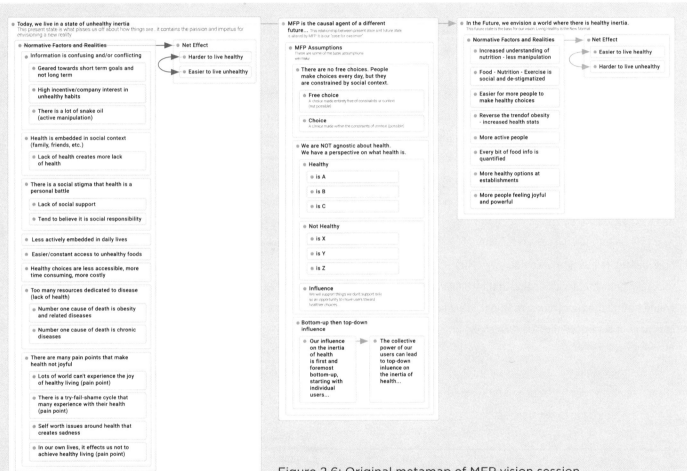

Figure 2.6: Original metamap of MFP vision session

state of affairs (that which pisses you off) to the desired future state (the basis for your vision). Truly visionary, the MFP team was bothered by the current state of affairs.

Today, we live in a state of unhealthy inertia. This present state is what pissed them off about how things were... it contained the passion and impetus for envisioning a new reality.

The current state included a number of terrible normative factors and realities, including health information that was confusing and/or conflicting, a lot of snake oil (active manipulation), the social stigma that health is a personal battle despite the fact that health is embedded in social context (family, friends, so forth), and less activity embedded in daily lives and easier/constant access to unhealthy foods, among others. The net effect of all of these norms and realities was that it was relatively easy to be unhealthy and much harder to be healthy.

MFP wanted to change these normative factors and realities—they envisioned a new normal. And they believed that they would be the company that would make that new normal a reality. In other words, they believed:

> MFP is the causal agent of a different future....This relationship between present state and future state is altered by MFP. It is our "case for existence."[46]

Here MFP took the time (something so many executive teams don't do) to think through the difficult questions and found answers for them. In the case for existence process, we call these "base assumptions"—things that you assume have an effect on lots of smaller decisions down the road.

- Did they have an opinion of what health was, or were they just purveyors of data? If they were not agnostic about what constituted health, what would they do if and when they were faced with the dilemma of supporting something that was less than ideal for a larger cause?

- Where is their greatest leverage point or influence? How does that influence play out strategically? MFP knew that their influence on the inertia of health was first and foremost bottom up, starting with individual users. But they also knew that the collective power of their users could lead to top-down influence on the inertia of health. They could actually use their data to change restaurant menus, gym policies, and even local, state, and federal policies.

- And they even considered important questions of choice and free will, given that their company was based on some assumption of where choices lie.

It was an amazing thing to watch these Silicon Valley entrepreneurs talking like founding fathers or academics, exploring the deep issues that their existence would cause them to face and need them to answer. Plato said, "Well begun is half done." These visionary entrepreneurs were laying down the solid foundation for a successful company. They were truly visionary, because they stepped into a future that didn't exist and looked around and then decided to build what they saw there: A totally new normal in which healthy living was the norm rather than the exception.

> In the Future, we envision a world where there is healthy inertia. This future state is the basis for our Vision: Living Healthy Is the New Normal.

They envisioned a world in which various factors and realities were the norm with the net effect that to live healthy was easier than to live unhealthy. We were mesmerized by their process and their visionary thinking. It was motivating just to be in the room with these folks. They saw their data in a way that could change lives for the better. At one point, it dawned on us that we suddenly felt love for this company. Their vision was so visionary, so passionate, so motivating, so compelling. At one point, we actually had the thought that we should just close up shop and work for them because their vision of a new and better world was that motivating.

Check #3: Our Vision Is Short and Simple

Perhaps the fastest way to tell if an organization has an ineffective vision or a good one is its length and degree of complexity. Harvard Business School professor and author John Kotter writes, "What's the 'golden rule' when crafting the vision statement? It should require effort to create, but should not require effort to understand—externally (customers) and especially internally (employees)."[47] We suggest applying the "nine-year-old test." Your vision should be short and simple enough to be understood by a nine-year old. You will appreciate the clarity that accompanies such a vision when you must teach it to your employees, and everyone else will appreciate it when its clarity provides guidance in every work situation.

A favorite in the short and simple vision department comes from Nike in the 1960s: Crush Adidas. Nestlé went an alternate route, which entailed 229 words.

> People understand that food is a source of nourishment and satisfaction, but also pleasure, health, happiness and peace of mind. They are increasingly aware that their food and beverage choices can impact their quality of life and affect the lives of others. Innovation has been at the heart of our company since its beginning. Ever since Henri Nestlé invented Farine Lactée to alleviate infant

mortality, we have been dedicated to enhance people's lives. Each day we strive to make our products tastier and healthier choices that help consumers care for themselves and their families. This would not be possible without our unmatched R&D capability, nutrition science and passion for quality in everything we do. We have the largest R&D network of any food company in the world, with 34 R&D facilities (3 Science & Research centres and 31 Product Technology Centres and R&D centres worldwide), and over 5,000 people involved in R&D. Behind every one of Nestlé's products there is a team of scientists, engineers, nutritionists, designers, regulatory specialists and consumer care representatives dedicated to earn our consumers' trust with safe products of the highest quality: at Nestlé, safety and quality are non-negotiable. Whether it is in terms of convenience, health or pleasure, we are able and committed to create trustworthy products, systems and services that contribute to improving the quality of consumers' lives.[48]

Remember that the vision is a mental model (not a statement), and think of the difficulties that attend getting a group to understand a complex, convoluted, and lengthy statement. We suggest applying the "9-year-old test."

Does that pass the "9-year-old test"? Remember that simple rules, followed by individuals, produce complex organizational behavior. Those simple rules must align with the organizational vision—the desired future goal or state. As a leader, you need to ensure that everyone knows the vision by heart. Even the most ardently engaged employee could not be expected to memorize, let alone internalize, such a vision statement.

Write down your vision, with a few extra sentences of explanation

Explain it to a 9 year-old.

Did they get it?

☐ Yes

☐ No

Activity 2.3: Visions should pass the "9-year-old test"

Check #4: Our Vision Is Measurable, Ideally Binary

A vision is a future state, but a clear one to which we can aspire and direct our efforts and strategies. We need to know where we are with respect to the vision. Are we making progress? Is it slipping away? Are we stuck? This leads to our next rule: visions must be measurable. Why is measurability important? A measurable vision enables you to determine whether you've achieved it.

There are lots of different ways to measure a vision, including taking into account multiple metrics. Your vision might end up being slightly more complex than "Eliminate email from the workplace," but the point is that you devise some way to determine whether you have arrived at your vision. For example, perhaps it is impossible to eradicate something completely, but a practical goal is to reduce it by 85%. That is a binary statement because it either true or false: it is or is not reduced 85%. "Eradicate homelessness among American veterans" is an effective vision.[49] "Decrease veteran homelessness by 85% in the United States" is an effective vision. "Improve homelessness among US veterans" is an ineffective vision because it's just not measurable.

Ideally, you are able to choose a vision that is binary—which is sort of measurability for dummies. A binary vision is great because you can't accidentally or unknowingly achieve it (or fail). Finishing a marathon is a good example—you either crossed the finish line, completing 26.2 miles, or you did not. The desired future state either currently exists or it does not. I'm either standing on the summit or I'm not. AIDS is either eradicated from Africa or it's not. We've either surpassed Amazon for online sales or we haven't. Here's a great binary vision from the Alzheimer's Association: "A world without Alzheimer's disease."

Of all of the rules for creating a great vision, choosing one that's binary poses the most problems for people. And it is true that you can create a workable vision that passes all of the other rules but not this one. It is difficult for folks to arrive at a vision they admire that is binary. "Living Healthy Is the New Normal" is binary, because a norm can be established quantitatively. It doesn't mean that achieving that vision is going to be easy, it's not. But it is binary. You'll know whether or not, or to what degree, you've achieved it. Summiting is binary. A Catholic World is binary. Life is binary. The value of pushing through to try to make your vision binary will pay off in the end, but it doesn't always occur with the first attempt. Many groups have created a vision they love that meets all of the criteria, except it's not entirely binary. That's okay. Work at it. Let the binary rule be a thorn in your side and push yourself to keep working at it. When you do finally achieve a completely binary goal, you'll understand its importance—it makes the goal of the organization imminently measurable, final, and crystal clear. You either made it or you didn't. A world free of malaria... AIDS... Alzheimer's... cancer—those are all binary visions. They are truly visionary as a result. None of those things are easy. All of them are grand and audacious statements. That's what makes them visionary. Of course, just because a vision is binary doesn't mean there is only one point of measure. Indeed, the opposite is true: because it is binary, it gives you an ongoing measure. Because the summit of Mount Everest stands at a binary 29,029 feet (8848 m), we can assess that 28,000 feet is better than 25,503 feet, which is better than 25,501 feet.

Be binary about whether your current vision is binary or not. If it isn't, keep using it and let the fact that it is not quite binary motivate you to do better. When you have the aha! moment and discover a version of it that is binary, you'll be glad you did.

Binary or not, visions should be measurable. There is some subtlety here, as well. "A World Free of Malaria" is a measurable vision. Not only is the binary malaria/no malaria point measurable, but we can measure malaria rates and deaths as they decrease from today's numbers (212 million cases, 429,000 deaths globally) to that zero point. If your vision includes numbers of cases of AIDS, or things like that, then measurability won't be a problem. But what if your vision is something that is less immediately measurable?

Living Healthy Is the New Normal

How do you make that measurable? Binary? Well, let's see how the innovators at MFP did it.

First, let's break down the vision into parts. The MFP crew broke it down into two elemental parts: [Living Healthy] and [New Normal]. Next, they defined what they meant by living healthy. They did so from the perspective of their app and the things that could be measured. For example, what they called Healthy Behavior Choices (or HBCs) included regular exercise, balanced diet, healthy weight, and alignment with user defined goals. All of these were defined by what a user logged in the app.

Figure 2.7: Listing the measures for each element of your vision

Then, the MFP team needed to define the new normal. A norm is something that we can establish quantitatively by obtaining data from a large, randomly selected, representative sample of the wider population. The wider population is, globally speaking, 7 billion people and growing, 300 million in the United States. So this population number can be staged. Because MFP had more than 80 million users of their health behaviors mobile app (at the time; it's much larger now), they had a data set larger and more specific than most, if not all, of the other researchers in the area combined. So, they simply needed to establish a standard for what the "new normal" would be. But they also wanted to eventually look at not just the user logs, but also the top-down influences they had, for example, on the normative behavior of restaurants in terms of their HBCs (portion size, farm to table, dietary balance, etc). Using this mental model, MFP took a vision that didn't immediately scream "I'm measurable" and found ways to measure it.

Sometimes you're going to think of ways to measure your vision (or mission) that you don't yet have the capacity for. That's okay. As long as your vision is measurable (hypothetically speaking), it passes the criterion. Whether you have the skills or present abilities to measure it is a capacity issue that can be dealt with later. And, even if you do have the capacity to measure your vision right away, you can always get better (more refined) at measuring it in the future.

Here are the elements of our vision...	Here's how we will measure them...	This vision can be completed/finished (i.e., it is binary)
An AIDS-free Africa	AIDS-free: measured by no existing or new cases of HIV or AIDS Africa: the entire continent	[X] Yes [ ] No
Your turn:	Your turn:	[ ] Yes [ ] No

Activity 2.4: Visions should be measurable

Check #5: Our Vision Lives in Hearts and Minds

The fifth check is at least as important as all the others. In fact, if you follow checks 1 through 4, it makes following check 5 much easier. Your job as a leader is to infuse your organization's culture into your staff, and it starts with ensuring that the vision is emblazoned in the neurons of every mind in the organization. The first step in doing so is remembering that the vision is not a statement, it's a mental model that needs to be built by everyone in the organization.

Interestingly enough, Monster.com gets it right, stating it plainly and simply: "Comparatively speaking, executives spend entirely too much precious time and energy crafting precisely worded company mission, vision, and value statements. This is time and effort they should be investing in making darned sure every human being on their payroll truly understands and appreciates what all that stuff means."[50]

That could not be truer of the vision, the cornerstone of your culture. Don't be fooled into thinking this is unimportant because it is the last rule. It's last because you need formulate the vision before you can enculturate it. But if you don't plan to engage in culture building—sharing mental models across your organization—you might as well save time and skip steps 1 through 4.

When we help people create a vision, one of the distinctions we make is between the vision statement, the vision logo, and the vision mental model. The vision statement is a string of words that describes the vision. Lots of people equate their vision with the words on the page. Others believe that the words on the page have meanings derived from the dictionary. Rather, the meaning of the vision statement is very specific and represents shared meaning within your company.[51] In comparison, the vision logo is an iconic image that captures the vision.

The actual vision is a mental model—a deep understanding of what your collective promised land looks like. We can't emphasize this enough. Your vision is the most important part of your organization's culture—the mental model that needs to be built by all. A vision statement can be "shared" in the sense of distributed verbally or electronically to all members. But your company will only have a true vision when it is enculturated among members. There's an easy way to assess this. Let's call it a vision test.

Your vision is the most important part of your organization's culture—the mental model that needs to be built by all.

THE VISION TEST

We'll often approach the leader of an organization who has asked for our help and administer a quick vision test.

Us: "Do you have a vision?"

CEO (emphatically): "Yes!"

Us: "Oh, okay, what is it?"

CEO: "Well, um...well it starts with how we are, um...well it says that..." (flags down subordinate to procure the vision)

Us: "Okay, that was instructive. What would we hear if we asked the next person who comes down the hall what your vision is?"

CEO: "Well, I think you'd hear our vision."

Us (grabbing an unsuspecting employee passing by): "Excuse me, what is your company's vision?"

Employee (hesitantly): "Um, it's, well it's something about how...it's on our website. It's also on the wall in the waiting room, do you mind if I go get it?"

We thank them and let them go about their business; we made our point. CEOs don't like it when we do that. But they do get the point: They don't have a vision. They have a bunch of words in a frame on the wall or on their website, which does not a vision make. They don't have a shared mental model of purpose residing in the hearts and minds of every member of the organization.

Figure 2.8: The vision test

Words on a page are not powerful until they live in the hearts and minds of people. As illustrated in Figure 2.8, visions are not the words that exist in frames on a wall or on the company website. In short, you must differentiate the vision (insight into what the future can be) from the vision statement (a written formulation of the vision) from the vision logo (a visual formulation of the vision). This is not rocket science. But this understanding will change you as a leader, change your daily behavior, and change your organization dramatically.

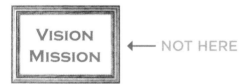

Figure 2.9: Where vision *must* reside

The MFP vision was created by two executives and their team who thought deeply about an upsetting situation and how it needed to change. The map in Figure 2.6 captures their process, which was not only critical for the executive team, but also for employees to understand their simplified mental model of vision. The vision statement, "Living Healthy is the New Normal" is simple and understandable. It is intrinsically motivating. It is measurable (as shown in the metamap) and it paints a vivid portrait of a future state.

Enculturating vision internally requires communicating in all of the ways that an external marketing campaign might launch a new product. When you see a Coca-Cola logo, you likely think lots of comfortable, joyful, American, refreshing, friendship-laden thoughts; similarly when people in your organization see the simplified vision statement or logo, you want them to think of the elaborated vision mental model—the whole concept, in all of its powerful, motivating glory. Figure 2.10 shows MFP's first vision logo used to connect the external brand (the leaping dancer logo) to the internal vision (the normal bell curve).

Figure 2.10: Early internal marketing for the vision

Enculturating the vision involves leadership. It entails helping people see something new—a possible future, a better place—and causing them to jettison their current activities and set off for a new goal. It's not something that occurs in the beginning and then subsides. We need leadership whenever someone doesn't see what's possible and, therefore, isn't joining the movement toward it, or when someone who is part of the movement grows weary or loses sight of the vision. The leader is the one who regroups and reinforces the vision—points to the icon or logo, repeats the slogan, and otherwise invokes the mental model that has a deep and abiding meaning to the group—and gets the weary ones moving again. Prolific business author Tony Schwartz similarly explains that leaders today must be.

> Chief Energy Officers, responsible for mobilizing, focusing, inspiring, and regularly recharging the energy of those they lead. … the best leaders define a clear and compelling vision and a set of values that inspire team members – while serving themselves as role models who walk their talk.

As Harvard Business School professor and leading expert on innovation Clay Christensen has tweeted: "Purpose must be deliberately conceived and chosen, and then pursued."[52]

We have had a lot of success helping our clients craft their visions. But we'll be honest: Some of our CEOs are so gleeful at finally defining a vision that, like children with birthday cake, they grab and go! We don't think that's a bad thing because the CEO can finally succinctly and accurately communicate what has been in his mind (in a more convoluted form) for so long. He's so thrilled that it finally exists

that he wants to move on and get to work with this new clarity. But one person's clarity does not a culture make. When a CEO grabs his shiny new vision and takes off like Gollum in Lord of the Rings, we always feel a little sadness because we know that he won't quite get the full value of his hard work.

Enculturating vision internally requires communicating in all of the ways that an external marketing campaign might launch a new product.

But when a CEO grabs her vision and sees it as a flag to be brought back to the organization and embedded as the centerpiece of the organization's culture, then we know everything is going to play out in a positive way for her. Her work isn't done until this mental model is woven into the cultural tapestry of the organization, until every person in the organization has had time to process and build the vision in their mind and their heart. Try this with employees while you are walking around:

Can the employee recite the vision statement verbatim?	How well can the employee explain what the vision statement means?	How well can the employee explain how the mission guides their daily work?
☐ Yes ☐ No	3 Above Average 2 Average 1 Below Average	3 Above Average 2 Average 1 Below Average

Activity 2.5: Visions live in hearts and minds

CONCLUSION

Wait a minute. Did you read that last "Visions must be enculturated" bit and think, "But I'm not *that* kind of leader. I'm introverted. I'm no Steve Ballmer!"?[53] Let's get something straight. What's a visionary? One who sees a picture of the future that others initially can't. What's a leader? One who gets others to see it and follow him or her to that place.

It is the power of the vision, the *shared mental model*, that drives an organization. Charisma, charm, even social influence won't enable a CEO to properly lead if he or she lacks vision. Collins and Porras dispel a common management myth.

> The function of a leader—the one universal requirement of effective leadership—is to catalyze a clear and shared vision of the organization and to secure commitment to and vigorous pursuit of that vision.[54]

Yes, this entails dogged commitment and perseverance on your part. Kulturenvy founder Corey McAveeney, writing in *Wired*, gets it right: "If you don't know why you get out of bed each day to go to work, neither will anyone else. Tell everyone what you value, why you value it, and make sure you actively follow through by acting upon it."[55]

Let's review the rules for creating a vision.

These rules will guide your work on the vision, which is your first priority as a leader. They will help you craft the keystone of your culture. It is the vision that provides the direction for all your work. It is the vision with which all systems, all activities, and all strategies must align. The future goal or state you envision for your organization is, after all, an emergent property of your everyday activity. So now you can proceed to enumerate the steps—the natural organizational function called *mission*—that, in repetition, achieves your vision.

CHECK	1	**Our vision depicts a desired future state**
CHECK	2	**Our vision is intrinsically motivating**
CHECK	3	**Our vision is short and simple**
CHECK	4	**We measure our vision**
CHECK	5	**We ensure our vision lives in hearts and minds**

Figure 2.11: Checks for a well-designed vision

CHAPTER 3 DO MISSION (M)

CHECK 1   Our vision depicts a desired future state

CHECK 2   Our vision is intrinsically motivating

CHECK 3   Our vision is short and simple

CHECK 4   We measure our vision

CHECK 5   We ensure our vision lives in hearts and minds

CHECK 6   **Our mission is action(s) done repeatedly**

CHECK 7   **Our mission brings about our vision**

CHECK 8   **Our mission explains WHO does WHAT for WHOM**

CHECK 9   **Our mission is clear, concise, and easily understood**

CHECK 10   **We measure our mission**

CHECK 11   **We ensure our mission lives in hearts and minds**

CHECK 12   **We ensure that mission moments are sacrosanct**

CHECK 13   We build capacity in order to do our mission

CHECK 14   We build capacity through a system of systems

CHECK 15   We map capacity to understand and better design systems

CHECK 16   We use learning to expand our capacity

CHECK 17   We harness the power of mental models

CHECK 18   We train people to think in order to learn

CHECK 19   We constantly evolve our mental models

CHECK 20   We create a culture of vision, mission, capacity, and learning

DO MISSION (M)

Vision without action is a daydream.
Action with without vision is a nightmare.
— Japanese proverb

Mission Statement: A long awkward sentence that demonstrates management's inability to think clearly.
— Scott Adams[1]

You know you need a vision—a future goal to aim for, an umbrella to align all your business activities under, a mental model to help inspire and guide every member of your organization on a daily basis. If vision is the future you see, mission is what you do—the actions you take, repeatedly—to bring about that future. Just as every organization has a vision—it is moving toward a future state, whether deliberately or not—every organization possesses a mission—it repeats some actions that advance it toward the vision. We want you to leverage these natural functions, to consciously decide them, optimally formulate them, and then enculturate them into your organization. In this chapter, we will

1. Address the immense confusion that surrounds corporate mission statements.

2. Explain the very serious consequences of this confusion, including the pervasive tendency to dismiss, disregard, or disrespect organizational missions.

3. Discuss whether the mission should be directed principally inward or outward. In other words, is the mission statement an internal or external communication?

4. Convey a mission's importance and value for organizations.

5. Give you rules for creating a successful mission (including the necessity of enculturating that mission).

6. Discuss the importance of mission moments, real-life instances of your mission that involve your customers.

At the broadest level, we're determined to rescue *mission* as a concept and managerial tool and explain its relation to leadership. More concretely, this chapter enables you to capitalize on your great new vision and translate that into concrete steps that your organization must execute repeatedly. We'll also discuss the ongoing but critical task of enculturating the mental model of mission in your organization.

HOW COULD WE GO SO WRONG WITH SOMETHING SO IMPORTANT?

There's a reason that there are articles in Inc. titled "The 9 Worst Mission Statements of All Time" and "Why Most Mission Statements Suck So Bad."[2] Weird Al Yankovic has a song titled "Mission Statement"[3] (using biz jargon from the statements of real companies). A Google search for "mission statement cartoon" yields 4,600,000 results (without even specifying images). The Google search "I hate mission statements" returns about 398,000 results. It is near obligatory when discussing mission statements (even among proponents) to point out their shortcomings.

- "Ninety-nine percent of the mission statements out there are useless."[4]

- "...if you want to read some good fiction and wonder what the heck some departments think their purpose is, check out random department websites and look at some mission statements."[5]

- "[Mission statements] are the product of untold man-hours of 'brainstorming' and 'focus-grouping' resulting in the blandest, most generalized, least potentially offensive, frequently asinine copy that could have been created by any group of monkeys in any boardroom in America."[6]

Figure 3.1: Are we trying to make them bad?[7]

What should we expect when missionstatements.com will draft a mission statement within 24 hours for your organization for $35. Their five-step wizard asks questions like, "What are some specific actions that your company has taken (or will take) that makes a significant difference to your customers?"[8] Although we think there are rules that should guide the creation of a mission, the formulaic, borderline-meaningless, dime-a-dozen mission statements out there are giving the idea of mission—which is essential to every organization—a bad name.

This is both tragic and dangerous. We're with Peter Drucker, who wrote, "that business purpose and business mission are so rarely given adequate thought is perhaps the most important cause of business frustration and failure."[9]

Mission Confusion Abounds!

Starting in the 1980s, there was tremendous pressure to create a mission statement (some blame Drucker, who was so right about so many things, for encouraging them). The job of creating these statements was often relegated to a small group of individuals or outsourced to consultants. Neither process was particularly conducive to innovation, originality, or realism. There was pressure to create something, but no one was really clear about why it should be created. The process was self-conscious, in that leaders probably were concerned more with "how it reads" than "what it means," let alone "why am I doing this?" Not to mention that there has never really been clarity or agreement about what a mission statement is, what it should do, and what belongs in it.

When it comes to mission statements, the experts disagree about fundamental things like purpose, audience, and content. Here's a good example (just one of several dozen) of mission-making instructions that radically miss the mark. A business consultant, CEO, and author wrote a piece in the *Huffington Post* titled "Is Your Business Confused?" explaining the importance of writing a mission statement for your company.

The author offers "a few essentials" for any mission statement.

- The purpose and aim of your organization (i.e., a definition of what your company is and does)
- The products and/or services your company offers
- What your company aspires to be
- What features/characteristics distinguish your company from its competitors
- Your company's core ideology, values, purpose, and visionary goals[10]

Other prescriptions are vague in a way that leaves the reader unclear about what they should write. Jeffrey Abrahams, author of *The Mission Statement Book*, describes a mission statement as "a declaration of the company's purpose…the mission statement brands the business and hopefully differentiates it from the competition so that customers understand that the company is committed to a purpose and will back that up with products and service."[11]

CHAPTER 3 Do Mission (M)   61

Figure 3.2: All too real...[12]

This is in contrast to the Army's version of a Mission, which communicates the "5W's:"

Who: the people involved, across the scale from organization to division to department to team;

What: the unit's essential task and type of operation;

When: the time given in the battalion operation order;

Where: the location stated in the mission; and

Why: the company purpose, taken from the leader's concept of the operation.

These elements guide the "actions" that comprise the stated mission. Military operations are executed through a mission order to accomplish a mission - which at times sounds more like a corporate vision (e. g.,"take that territory"). Generally speaking, successful missions are the result of clear articulation and execution of all elements of the mission as stated by the commander. "Under mission command, commanders provide subordinates with a mission, their commander's intent, a concept of the operations, and resources adequate to accomplish the mission. They leave the details of execution to their subordinates and expect them to use initiative and judgment to accomplish the mission."

While the U.S. military has a clearly communicated understanding of a mission, the study of corporate missions is plagued by a lack of consensus on and clarity about key terms and the object of analysis itself.[13] For example, one study described 23 years of research that used definitions of mission statements composed of widely varying items (as many as 10 items in one definition). As is the case in many fields where our knowledge is nascent, inconsistency in defining the object of study hinders progress. The authors write, "there appears to be virtually no consensus as to what mission statements should or should not include." Table 3.1 shows the authors' summary of the "content" of mission from key works on the subject.[14]

MISSION STATEMENTS AND FIRM PERFORMANCE

Previous definitions/components of mission

MISSION COMPONENTS	Drucker (1974)	Want (1986)	Pearce & David (1987)	Campbell & Yeung (1991)	Collins & Porras (1991)	Coates et. al. (1991)	Klemm et. al. (1991)	Ireland & Hitt (1992)
Purpose/raison d'etre	X	X		X			X	X
Values/beliefs/philosophy		X	X	X				X
Business strategy/distinctive competence/competitive position	X			X			X	X
Behavior standards & policies		X		X				
Corporate level aims/goals		X			X	X	X	
Self-concept/identity		X	X					
Public image			X					
Location			X					
Technology			X					
Concern for survival			X					

Table 3.1: Components of different mission definitions

Yet there is hope! Not every business consultant or company or expert is confused on the subject of mission. Many folks are, at least in many respects, getting it right. Leanne Hoagland-Smith, a consultant in the area of organizational culture, makes a valuable etymological point.

A vision in its earliest definition means to see and has been translated into the act or power of seeing…

Now mission is entirely different. From its Latin origins it means to send, not see. Mission therefore implies action. For action to have value it must be measurable and directly connected to the power of seeing. Without the measurement, the old expression rings true, if you cannot measure it, you cannot manage it.[15]

Why Do I Need a Mission?

Why does your organization need a mission? How else does any collective know what's best to do? In an article called "Why I Hate Mission Statements But Love Missions," business author and consultant Brad Federman explains that missions guide organizations into "real action." Identifying the most important quality, "missions are known," he explains: "Think about it: would you send a group of soldiers into a conflict without a mission or without them knowing the mission? No way. But most organizations do just that."[16]

The importance of a mission has only increased over time, as we navigate a knowledge economy in a complex world and come to appreciate that all organizations are complex adaptive systems. Training manager Michael Emery explains that missions promote discussions about "who the team is, what the team does, and why they do it." The definition of what the team does, does not compose a detailed instruction manual. He writes:

When there is a clear team mission, members know what to do in unexpected situations. At best, a mission statement provides powerful principles for individual and group performance. These are increasingly important issues as companies continue to evolve from control-related strategies to individual behavior management. This is true regardless of what evolution occurs—TQM, self-directed work teams, or even participative management.[17]

The actions prescribed by the mission are its simple rules. We can't plan for every contingency so we need agents who have rules to guide their on-the-spot decision making and behavior.

We face problems in trying to estimate the effects of missions and their characteristics on organizational outcomes. The definitions employed by academics, consultants, practitioner-scholars, and organizational leaders vary in consequential and substantive ways. Many definitions of mission pack in several discrete phenomena (e.g., corporate standards, strategy, philosophy, values, rationale for existence). We'd be comparing oranges and apples, at best.

Nonetheless, there are some data. A large international study on workers' quality of life on the job reported the following about the importance of mission: "Only 34% felt a connection to their company's mission, and those who didn't feel such a connection were 62% less likely to stay with their employers and 45% less engaged." The vision and mission of an organization jointly formed the greatest factor influencing employee job satisfaction and intent to stay.[18] This disconnect fuels what all CEOs dread: disengagement. Reporting on the state of the American workplace in 2013, Gallup wrote about the associated costs.

> The vast majority of U.S. workers, 70%, are "not engaged" or "actively disengaged" at work, meaning they are emotionally disconnected from their workplace and are less likely to be productive. Actively disengaged employees alone cost the U.S. between $450 billion to $550 billion each year in lost productivity, and are more likely than engaged employees to steal from their companies, negatively influence their coworkers, miss workdays, and drive customers away.[19]

What academic studies there are on the effects of mission statements have provided weak and ambiguous results.[20] One study found that mission indirectly affected financial performance. Its effect was indirect: the level of employee commitment to the mission and the "degree to which an organization aligns its internal structure, policies and procedures with its mission" both were positively related with employee behavior. Employee behavior, in turn, was directly related to financial performance.[21]

In the previous chapter, we discussed the fact that meaning and purpose are fundamental human needs. Harvard psy-chologist Amy Cuddy is an expert in human behavior and motivation. Her work, while focused on individual goals, can help us understand the importance of mission. Cuddy argues that "The biggest mistake a lot of people make in setting goals... is that they focus only on the outcome, not the process." She explains that big goals (like a corporate vision) can be overwhelming, considering the number of steps along the way to the goal (each of which might bring failure). Her advice is to instead learn to "embrace the process" (love and live the mission, we would say), since much research shows that focusing on incremental change increases performance.[22] So, yes, create an inspirational vision that gets everyone out of bed and excites them about the future, but ground them in the mission. Luke Arthur argues that having a clear mission that everyone in the company understands "is a sign of a potentially strong culture. Many successful companies know what they are trying to accomplish and are moving in a clear direction."[23]

Crafting a Great Mission

Missions are, first and foremost, the action(s) you repeatedly take to bring about the vision. Hence vision and mission *must align*. Your mission should be short and simple (hence easily understood), as well as measurable. Finally, as with all VMCL functions, missions *must be enculturated*.

Before we articulate these rules, we need to discuss the audience for your mission. Is your mission statement an internal or external communication? Strategic management or public relations? Indeed, one of the most frequent questions we receive from organizational leaders is whether the mission and vision are for internal or external consumption. The mission, in simplest terms, is the actions you repeatedly perform to bring about the vision. The mission is first and foremost an internal document for transforming (or forming) an adaptive, effective, and powerful organization of systems thinkers. However, a carefully crafted and effective mission and vision (not to mention values, and other aspects of your capacity) will by extension be attractive to those outside your organization as well, including potential employees.

The mission, in simplest terms, is the actions you repeatedly perform to bring about the vision.

Throughout the section explaining the rules for crafting mission, we will present corporate mission statements that fulfill particular rules (or parts of rules). As you will see, many missions heed one rule while disregarding the others.

Check #6: Our Mission Is Action(s) Done Repeatedly

The mission statement has a specific function: it targets action.
—Thomas J. Roach[24]

Let's examine the the word *repeatedly*. This signals that missions aren't something we do once. A mission is an algorithm for doing something over and over again. As Will Durant puts it: "We are what we repeatedly do. Excellence, then, is not an act, but a habit."[25] This notion is related to our concept of a complex adaptive system (simple rules) and the idea that your efficiencies (and profitability) will come from developing the capacity to do the same thing over and over (akin to process-based "economies of scale"). Mission is the thing your employees (autonomous agents) do every day that will produce the organizational behavior that, in turn, will eventually achieve your vision. The mission of your organization is the collection of simple rules that direct the complex system.

With respect to specifying repeated actions in a mission, Google does pretty darn well: "To organize the world's information and make it universally accessible and useful." Patagonia is a company recognized for its social responsibility.[26] Their mission statement also does well in specifying the actions the company repeatedly performs:

"Build the best product, cause no unnecessary harm, use business to inspire,[27] and implement solutions to the environmental crisis."[28] Although Patagonia does articulate a three-paragraph statement of "Our Reason for Being" below the mission statement, we think they'd also benefit from developing a short and inspirational vision statement. Carillion—"a leading international integrated support services business"—went off the rails with their mission: "Carillion's strategy is derived from our mission to make tomorrow a better place."[29] That's not a repeated step: That's a (hard-to-measure) vision unto itself!

This does raise an interesting point and a cautionary note in the evaluation of mission statements. Because the primary audience is internal and because the mission is a mental model, we can't be sure how a given company interprets the words of their mission statement. We encountered an example when writing this chapter. Both of us love quotes, and often pile them at the top of the Google Doc for every chapter. Derek added the quote "Do Your Job," which he found inspiring, and attributed it to the New England Patriots. On seeing this, Laura fought the impulse to hit the delete key and instead asked Derek to provide clarification for a quote that she found neither informative nor inspirational.

> Mission is the thing your employees do every day that will produce the organizational behavior that, in turn, will eventually achieve your vision.

It turns out Derek was furnishing the mission statement of the Patriots. He wrote in the comments, "The message is, you always have a job to do, so do it. This simple mission is universally and readily applicable to any and all roles in the Patriots organization, positions on the field, or situations that require adaptation." Still confused, Laura got Derek to explain more concretely, including how Do Your Job meant receivers might (adaptively) engage in downfield blocking as appropriate. As one commentator wrote, "New England's receivers just didn't decide to start blocking this game. The idea of Do Your Job is a constant reminder in the facility, so everything is done with that in mind. The offseason program, the weight room, how you watch film, etc."[30] Do Your Job means exemplary performance every time in every task, even if it's not your typical assignment, in your comfort zone, or your particular forté.

Some experts recommend that the mission be inspirational and a mechanism for distinguishing oneself from close competitors. As you might have guessed by now, we think this is not requisite for a mission (which describes repeated actions that produce the vision).[31] Look—for too long too many organizations have thrown too many things into their mission statements. Sometimes, probably most of the time, less is more. The mission is what you DO. In fact, from working with hundreds of organizations, we have found that the more similar the organizations, either in category or in purpose, the more similar will be their missions. (This does not apply to visions, which exhibit greater variation across organizations.) Once again, though, we must remember that missions, like visions, are mental models. So while different organizations may use the same words in their missions, the meaning of those words might vary greatly. It is the meaning behind the words that matters.

Check #7: Our Mission Brings About Our Vision

This is unbelievably important. Let's find different ways to make the point, first being visual.

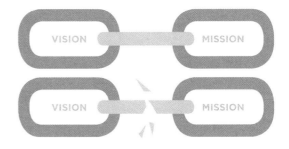

Figure 3.3: Aligned versus unaligned vision and mission

Perhaps the easiest way to think of the relationship between vision and mission is: *mission and vision must align*. Your mission will be meaningless if it is not aligned with your vision (your organization's North Star). You can also say that vision and mission must be coupled. Finally, we can return to our understanding that simples rules produce emergent phenomena in complex adaptive systems, and say: *vision is an emergent property of the mission*.

This rule is very important and we will return to alignment again and again. So much of leadership is about alignment, and it all starts with aligning your mission to your vision. We'll let others corroborate the point.

"Building a visionary company requires one percent vision and 99 percent alignment." —Jim Collins and Jerry Porras[32]

"Make your work to be in keeping with your purpose." —Leonardo da Vinci[33]

"You've got to think about big things while you're doing small things, so that all the small things go in the right direction." —Alvin Toffler[34]

"No company, small or large, can win over the long run without energized employees who believe in the [vision] and understand how to achieve it." —Jack Welch[35]

You can have a great vision and a great mission but together they can suck. This means that you need to pay careful attention to how your vision and mission match up. Basically, ask yourself the following question: if I ask ten smart, rational, reasonable people whether doing my mission repeatedly would eventually lead to my vision, what would they say? Better yet, test it out by asking those people! Visions and missions that are coupled work well together. They work in sync: the repeated doing of your mission should get you to your vision.

We often demonstrate alignment by giving the two noncorporate examples in Figure 3.4.

MISSION: Convert the unconverted   VISION: A Catholic world

MISSION: Go forth and multiply   VISION: Resilient biodiversity

Figure 3.4: Vision and mission alignment[36]

It's no secret that Walmart is vying for some of Amazon's e-commerce.[37] Walmart's website reads: "What Walmart can do that no one else can is marry e-commerce with our existing assets to deliver a seamless shopping experience at scale. That is our vision and our mission, and managing our portfolio is essential to accomplishing our goals."[38] So the Walmart mission and vision statements are:

Mission: Marry e-commerce with our existing assets.
Vision: A seamless shopping experience at scale.

Pretty good in the alignment department!

We have a personal alignment story, one about how vision begets a mission. Long before he and Laura started their research lab, Derek noticed that operating from an information paradigm was causing all kinds of problems. It angered him that people in organizations would talk about information sharing (via email, report, or CEO address) as if it meant that everybody was on board. The idea that "they understand because I covered that information" drove him nuts, as it conflates sharing information with the sharing of mental models. Information alone is not enough; we need to structure information to make it meaningful. And meaning is key to understanding. Here's Derek's vision: all organizations share meaningful mental models instead of just information. Figure 3.5 illustrates that the meaning of a vision can be captured in an icon or logo that makes it stick. In effect, the vision is the death of the information-sharing paradigm and the birth of a new paradigm of meaning-based mental models.

Figure 3.5: A vision logo

Derek knew he needed to connect this vision to a repeatable mission. He had already discovered DSRP (a powerful cog-

nitive grammar explained in Chapter 5) and a rudimentary "visual language" to structure information to create meaning. But he *envisioned* software that would make the user a better, more systematic thinker. He often made the analogy, "What if a word-processing program could make you a better writer?"

The mental models created in this software could be shared, collaborated on, and evolved. Much more than that, Derek and Laura envisioned a platform that would yield emergent properties beyond our imagination (e.g., organizational learning, the emergence of culture, engagement, innovation, and so forth). To truly bring about the "end of information," people all around the world would need to build, share, and evolve their mental models, and they would need a tool to help them do it. In their minds, mental model software was that tool and the mission was to facilitate and motivate building, sharing and evolving mental models. In other words:

- Mission: Facilitate and motivate building, sharing, and evolving mental models

- Vision: All organizations build and share mental models

The mission—done by many over a long time—will produce the vision.

Finally, aligning your mission to your vision serves a motivational and aspirational function. Exploring the benefits of mission statements, business professor Harsh Verma explains the importance of framing the mission's activities in terms of the vision.

> The job unless infused with higher order relevance remains a chore. It is something done for "them" but surely not for "self." But when a higher order connect is developed the job becomes an opportunity, a reward and a gift. The job needs to be transformed into a meaningful activity. Thus businesses have a challenge of appealing to its people both at lower level of sustenance and at a higher level of existence.[39]

The job of a vision is to ensure that everyone knows the goals of the organization. The job of a mission is to ensure that everyone knows the simple rules for bringing about the vision. Since vision and mission are co-workers, it's also their job to work well together. If the vision and mission are not performing their collective job duties, then they are ineffective. When we talk about vision and mission as a perfectly aligned, harmonious unit, we call it Vision-Mission.

Beyond alignment with the vision and specification of steps to achieve it, missions tell us three things (two whos and a what).

Check #8: Our Mission Explains WHO Does WHAT for WHOM

Your mission is first and foremost an internal-facing communication. Do not design your mission as an external marketing device. That said, a well-crafted mission statement explains who you are and what you do and for whom you do it, and in many instances that is something (in simplified form) you want the world to know. Here are three questions to help you brainstorm your mission, the shared mental model that will guide the activities of everyone in your organization.

1. What actions and activities must be repeatedly taken to bring about the vision?

2. Who are the individuals who must take these steps?

3. Who or what is served by the mission?

We've already addressed (1): the "what," or the simple steps of the mission. As for (2), the "who" (executes the mission) aspect—which is typically all organization members—could include other constituencies. It may seem obvious that you are talking to your staff or employees, but especially in this day and age where the boundaries between things are increasingly blurred, it is even more important to explicate in your mission who is being told to do what. For example, is Uber's mission providing instructions for their 10,000 employees or their 20,000 contractors or both? In numerous cases we've seen organizations significantly muddle these two "whos": who the mission is speaking to and who the mission serves.

Let's look at (3), who you perform the mission for. When you explicate for whom or what the mission is being done, that makes for an inherently customer-obsessed organization. Consider this who (or what), in simple terms, as your customer.[40] Being precise and explicit about who/what you serve is important because there is both intrinsic and extrinsic motivation that comes from grounding your work in *serving* others.[41] Specifying the who/what your mission serves also enables you to collect real-world feedback from your customers. If you don't know (or don't care) for whom/what you're doing your mission, then you'll likely never get their opinion on how you're doing. That's a recipe for imminent failure. You want your organization's mission to be unabashedly customer-obsessed. Not because customer-centrism is what everyone is talking about these days, nor because it's the ethical thing to do. Because you need the feedback.

> Your mission is first and foremost an internal-facing communication. Do not design your mission as an external marketing device.

Based on our work with numerous organizations, leaders sometimes conflate *who* needs to do the mission and *who* the mission serves. A surprising number of organizations (including ones with significant longevity) don't know who their customer is. Instead of directly serving a targeted (typically high-need) population, they do so indirectly through other service providers, *who are their actual customers*. Not recognizing who is served by the mission can create tremendous confusion. This faulty mental model may cause you to see direct service providers not as your customers but as proxy employees responsible for executing your mission. While these people (your customers) engage in direct service provision and expect help from your organization, you ironically expect them *to do your mission* and object when they don't. Rather than seeing them as customers and valuing their feedback and customer experience as critical to your success, you're frustrated that they aren't doing their job.

Having mistaken your customers (who you serve), you might also have never identified an appropriate mission. In the numerous organizations we've worked with that have suffered from this problem, we find that one simple question can expose it and begin to distinguish *who does the mission* from *whom the mission serves*. We ask, "Who do we directly interact with?" or "Do we actually interact directly with [constituency of interest and presumed customer]?" This does the trick.

This who/whom conflation problem isn't confined to nonprofits. Take Facebook, for example. We've all used Facebook for years and never paid them a cent for the value that they provide. This means that "we" are not Facebook's customers, even though it might seem like Facebook exists to serve its users. Facebook's customers are its advertisers. It turns out that we are actually Facebook's *product*. So delineating "who does what for whom" is an extremely important step in developing your mission.

Implied in the mission	This is the mission statement	Implied in the mission	Implied in the mission
Tells someone (this is almost always your employees)	To do something (add repeatable steps here)	In service of someone (customer) or something (cause)	To bring about your vision
Example: Tells employees	To facilitate and motivate healthy behavior choices	iPhone and Android App users	To bring about a world where living healthy is the new normal.
Your turn:	Your turn:	Your turn:	Your turn:

Activity 3.1: Outlining your mission

Check #9: Our Mission Is Clear, Concise, and Easily Understood

Because the mission first and foremost explains the steps that over time lead to the vision, and because the agents of a complex adaptive system (your organization) need to share mental models to be effective, clarity is non-negotiable. Concision generally is an aid to clarity. And clarity begets understanding. Most missions are long, wind-filled paragraphs, when instead they could be stated in a few words. They wax on poetically in flowery prose when they should be simple. Bad missions are paragraphs of platitudes; good missions are concise and obvious in their meaning. Remember the "9-year-old test" from last chapter? Yes, that applies to your mission, as well. If your average 9-year-old can't understand your mission, go back to the drawing board. Who knew 9-year-olds would be so important to your leadership?!

Contrasting style and substance, Michael Emery clarifies, "A mission statement is not about goals or the meaning of life."[42] Noting that most people articulate their ideas more clearly in verbal form, he suggests initially avoiding narrative expression and instead capturing key ideas in a bulleted list. Barnes & Noble offers a mission statement that is neither clear nor concise, and is frankly somewhat baffling.

> Our mission is to operate the best specialty retail business in America, regardless of the product we sell. Because the product we sell is books, our aspirations must be consistent with the promise and the ideals of the volumes which line our shelves. To say that our mission exists independent of the product we sell is to demean the importance and the distinction of being booksellers.
>
> As booksellers we are determined to be the very best in our business, regardless of the size, pedigree or inclinations of our competitors. We will continue to bring our industry nuances of style and approaches to bookselling which are consistent with our evolving aspirations.
>
> Above all, we expect to be a credit to the communities we serve, a valuable resource to our customers, and a place where our dedicated booksellers can grow and prosper. Toward this end we will not only listen to our customers and booksellers but embrace the idea that the Company is at their service.[43]

How do we all flock to that mission? How likely is it that we all have a shared understanding of it? How specifically does that mission guide or govern my day as a Barnes & Noble worker? What does all that text mean for my work? This mission is the opposite of clear and concise. It's genuinely hard to understand what it means, hence we don't know its implications (or how to answer these questions).

Let us offer an example of a mission (counterinsurgency) approach characterized by clarity and concision: "Clear. Hold. Build." But even that excellent mission statement didn't come easy. Figure 3.6 shows a multimillion dollar capacity map showing many feedback loops that was developed by the CIA and Pentagon for the war in Afghanistan.[44]

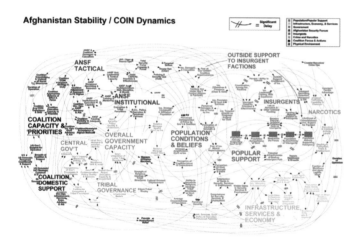

FIGURE 3.6: Afghanistan strategy map

General Stanley A. McChrystal, charged with implementing the map's strategy, remarked "No one can actually figure the darn thing out. When we understand that slide, we'll have won the war." Four-star General George W. Casey, Jr., a systems thinker who popularized the acronym VUCA, conveys the importance of honing one's message.

It's essential to distill a message into a few key points and hone its delivery. Clear communication is like sharpening a pencil: you slowly remove the unnecessary until you are left with a pointed, useful message. After trying and failing to communicate our strategy, we went back to the drawing board and came up with "Clear. Hold. Build." and re-communicated it. It was much better understood.[45]

Clear. Hold. Build. Now that's a clear mission (especially relative to the overwhelming complexity of the map in Figure 3.6).

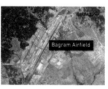

FIGURE 3.7: Agents and simple rules view

Figure 3.7 shows that General Casey's three-rule mission can be applied at multiple levels of scale across his organization (i.e., it is fractal). For example, a platoon of soldiers tasked with clearing a house can apply the mission to clear the house of dangers, then set up security measures to hold the house, and then build relationships in the house to ensure longer-term success. The mission is fractal in that at every level of scale, from the block that the house is on to the neighborhood, town, region, and eventually provinces, the military can use the same mission. Clear, hold, build this house. Clear, hold, build this village. Clear, hold, build this airport. Clear, hold, build this province. Clear, hold, build this country.

This is my mission with a few extra sentences of explanation

Explain it to a 9 year-old.

Did they get it?

☐ Yes

☐ No

Activity 3.2: Missions should pass the "9-year-old test"

Check #10: Our Mission Is Measurable

This means that each word or element in your mission can be measured in some way using a single metric or a set of metrics. We advise that people keep these metrics fairly simple. You likely don't need a differential equation. Most of the time some simple counts will do. Wal-Mart had the quintessential measurable mission statement in 1990: "Become a $125 billion company by the year 2000."[46] Though less convenient to measure, Ford's classic early mission to "democratize the automobile" could plausibly be quantified, perhaps with Ford vehicle ownership rates among all those people within one standard deviation above and below the median income level in the United States. More difficult to quantify would be Asana's big, hairy, audacious mission: "to help humanity thrive by enabling all teams to work together effortlessly."[47] Worst yet in terms of measurability is Coca-Cola's mission statement:

• To refresh the world...

• To inspire moments of optimism and happiness...

• To create value and make a difference.[48]

It's almost as if they included the ellipses as an acknowledgment of the whimsical nature of these "actions." We'd hate to be responsible for the mental acrobatics necessary to measure that stuff.

Let's return to General Casey's "Clear. Hold. Build." mission. We could choose to tie one or all of the following metrics to each part of the mission:

Parts of Casey's Mission	Examples of Metrics
Clear	Number of houses, blocks, streets, neighborhoods, towns cleared
Hold	Number of hours, days, weeks, months, years held
Build	Number of relationships, partnerships, coalitions, hospitals, infrastructural projects, service projects built

Table 3.2: Measuring the parts of a mission

Remember, too, the maxim "Not everything that can be counted counts and not everything that counts can be counted."[49] Especially for young organizations, precise and valid quantitative metrics may not exist yet. Some things may not be conducive to quantification. The important thing is that the ideas contained in your mission must be measurable. You may not have a customer inspiration survey designed just yet, but it is possible. If at first you don't have access to quantitative measures, use a qualitative proxy knowing that over time you will evolve more reliable measures.

Here are the elements of our mission	Here's how we'll measure them
Example: **Facilitate** and **motivate** healthy behavior choices	**Facilitate**: Number of daily active logins; Number of recommendations used; Click thru rate on searches **Motivate**: Number of friends; Number of streaks; Gamification analytics
Your turn:	Your turn:

Activity 3.3: Missions should be measurable

> The important thing is that the ideas contained in your mission must be measurable.

Remember why measurability matters: because feedback matters. We need to assess our progress on the path toward the vision, because a mission is, by definition, the incremental actions that over time get you there. If after consulting the metrics you find that following this path isn't getting you where you want to go, you either need to adjust the path or adjust the destination. Another possibility is that you have insufficiently inculcated the mental model of your mission and vision to your organization. This leads to our final mission check.

Check #11: Our Mission Lives in Hearts and Minds

> Tell them what you're going to tell them, tell them, then tell them what you told them.
> —communication axim[50]

> People often say that motivation doesn't last. Well, neither does bathing - that's why we recommend it daily. —Zig Ziglar[51]

As with your vision, if you take time to craft your mission thoughtfully—making it clear and concise so it's easy to understand, ensuring it explains concrete actions that lead to your vision—it will be much easier to enculturate. You can more readily ascertain if everyone shares—understands and endorses—this important mental model.

Imagine instead a three-paragraph mess of business jargon and platitudes. Who wants to do the heavy lifting of embedding that in your culture? Your mission, after all, should denote action. Referencing *Mission: Impossible*, Kevin McManus writes:

When a mission is meaningful and supported through complementary workplace systems and associated behaviors, people commit to the mission as a matter of course. Agent Phelps didn't need to write his mission down: It was OK that it self-destructed five seconds after he heard it. If all of the mission-decorated banners, mugs, and wall hangings were removed from your organization, would people still know what the mission is?[52]

As with all aspects of your culture—especially vision, capacity, and learning—we recommend mapping out your organization's mission using a visual map that conveys meaning. These maps visually depict not only the information, but the underlying structure that gives that information meaning. In Figure 3.8 you can see MyFitnessPal's mental model of their powerful two-part mission: *Facilitate. Motivate.*

Figure 3.8: Map of MyFitnessPal's mission

MyFitnessPal's mission cut through the chaos of their successful startup to identify the two critical things that would need to be repeated in order to bring about their audacious vision, Living Healthy Is the New Normal. These two elements—facilitate and motivate—are measurable and interrelated. They provide the company guidance on a daily basis for all work, including engineering and sales, talent management, and innovation.

All of the same things that you would do to sell to an outside customer you need to bring to bear as you realize that you have an inside customer and that your product is your vision-mission.

Gallup collects great data on employee engagement and aspects of strategic management and culture, and calculates costs associated with various organizational features or events. Their *Business Journal* features useful reports on their surveys. Although a 2014 report[53] about mission used a definition that more resembled vision (ultimate purpose), their advice for "maximizing mission-driven leadership" is apt for those seeking to embed the mission as a mental model in their culture. In particular, we'd suggest the following four of their recommended steps.

1. Ask your leadership team, "What do you get paid to do?" Listen for statements that reflect mission in their answers.
2. Ask colleagues to discuss when they have recently seen the company mission in action.
3. Coach leaders about how to use their strengths to advance the company mission.
4. Evaluate strategic objectives for this year, asking why each is a focus. How do they serve your mission?

And we would add one more simple idea to this list of things you can do to inculcate mission: *everything*. What we mean by everything is for you to think about enculturating mission (and vision) in the same way you think about attracting customers through external marketing and sales efforts. Your internal customers (employees and staff) can be taught using any and all of the strategies you use to evangelize and make the sale to outside customers. Have the design department create beautiful media for the mission and vision. Have creative work up event ideas to foster your mission. And, you need to pound the pavement and sell, sell, sell. All of the same things that you would do to sell to an outside customer you need to bring to bear as you realize that you have an inside customer. Your product is your Vision-Mission: the perfectly aligned, harmonious collaboration of vision and mission.

As with vision, "walking the talk" is extremely important. If, as a leader, your actions don't align with mission, how can you expect the same of your employees? You should align incentives (such as rewards and recognition) with the behaviors that most advance the mission. Continuously connect the mental models of mission and vision in as many ways and types of media as possible. The more thoroughly you enculturate your mission, the more you'll get (and ace!) what we call "mission moments" (which can then be valorized, publicized, and otherwise exploited to the max).

TRY THIS!

First, ask yourself: What is our vision and mission? Record your answers. Next, ask people in your organization the same question. See what they say. Pay attention.

- Did they use the specific words of the vision?
- What was their affect when reciting it: Positive? Negative? Like it was a chore? Or like it was something they were excited about?
- How different were their responses from one another and from how you would say it?

Once they are done, ask them some questions about what it all means. This will get beyond the recitation of the verbatim words of the statements and go deeper into the mental model they have built.

- Do they talk about important nuances of the vision and mission?
- Can they explain how to measure it?
- Are they passionate and excited by it?
- Do they deconstruct its subtleties and complexities and then roll it up into its simple form?
- Do they connect the mission to the vision?

The results of this activity should tell you if you have an effective vision (and mission). Don't be discouraged if you don't have a vision-mission yet.

Now you know that there is work to do and exactly how to do it. Set about creating your Vision-Mission using the rules and then try this activity again!

Can the employee recite the mission statement verbatim?	How well can the employee explain what the mission statement means?	How well can the employee explain how the mission guides their daily work?
☐ Yes ☐ No	3 Above Average 2 Average 1 Below Average	3 Above Average 2 Average 1 Below Average

Activity 3.4: Missions Live in Hearts and Minds

Check #12: Mission Moments Are Sacrosanct

Your mission is a mental model of what you repeatedly do to bring about the vision that guides your behavior 24/7. *Mission moments* emerge from this. They are precious instances of interaction, direct and indirect, with customers. Mission moments are an emergent property of repeated actions; they are your mission playing out in real life.

Mission moments should reign supreme in your organization. They are as precious as a baby hugging a puppy. Your organization lives and dies based on its mission moments, so they should be treated as such. Committing yourself and your organization to the sacred nature of mission moments will bring immense value and payoff, because mission moments matter in three ways.

1. Mission moments follow a simple equation: Do them well, get more opportunities to do them. Do them poorly, get fewer opportunities.
2. When a mission moment doesn't go well, this signals you are not doing your mission well (which may indicate a lack of capacity in your organization).
3. Mission moments are opportunities to get feedback from customers (i.e., engage in organizational learning).

Over the years our clients have found the idea of mission moments very useful. Appreciating mission moments requires making a distinction between the mission and a single instance of its fulfillment in real life. Your mission is a mental model shared by everyone in your organization that is reflected in the mission statement. Because your mission is something you do in service of customers it is also contained within every individual interaction your customer has with your organization (i.e., within mission moments).

Mission moments should reign supreme in your organization. They should be treated like a baby hugging a puppy, served on a gold tray in church.

A mission moment involves contact with your customer in some way. Although interacting with customers might not seem rare, because it happens every day, compared with the many other daily activities your organization performs, it is relatively rare. Consider, for example, all of the time a restaurant spends preparing for dinner service compared with the actual time restaurant staff engage directly with diners.

At the same time, mission moments needn't occur in real time or involve employee-customer contact. For example, a software engineer is guided by her mission to *facilitate* and *motivate* some customer behavior. Specifically, she writes the code for her cloud-based software that helps *facilitate* and *motivate* customers to share their expertise online, then uploads the code to go live at 4 PM. Having built capacity to do the mission, she goes home for the day.

Your customer, comfortably ensconced on the couch in his underwear at 3 AM, logs on and finds that the new code makes it easier (facilitates) or more motivating to share his expertise. That's the moment that matters—that 3 AM mission moment. What the coder did at 4 PM was capacity-building informed by the mission, which in turn improved the 3 AM mission moment (your customer's interaction with your user interface).

My mission statement is:	My mission moments happen when	How sacrosanct are mission moments in our culture?
Example: Facilitate and motivate healthy behavior choices	Users interact with the app or contact of any kind with the company	**3** Highly **2** Average **1** Not at all
Your turn:	Your turn:	

Activity 3.5: Differentiating mission from mission moments

CONCLUSION

Ask yourself: would I assemble people with diverse interests, life experiences, perspectives, personal goals, ingrained habits, temperaments, and loyalties under one roof without telling them why? Yes, vision is a natural function of any social group, but if you don't set the future goal, don't complain about the end state that emerges.

Next ask yourself: would I assemble said group and expect them to reach the desired future state (vision) without explicit instructions on how to get there? Yes, all organizations are complex adaptive systems, but you want to dictate (at least initially) the rules your agents should repeatedly follow. Complexity emerging from simplicity is beautiful in the abstract, but don't complain about where your organization ends up if you don't set those simple rules (mission).

Finally... and we just can't say this enough (as a matter of fact, we'll italicize it for even more emphasis): *visions and missions are mental models*. Vision statements and mission statements—unless they represent a shared understanding and some degree of endorsement and resonance among group members—are merely empty words.

As a leader, you need to see everything—time, meetings, rituals, communication, informal conversations, trainings, resources, social approval, and so forth—as an opportunities to teach vision and mission, assess understanding, reiterate vision and mission, find new and unusual ways to embody vision and mission, and assess emotional resonance and support for vision and mission. This sounds daunting, but you're not alone. Enlist your visionary leaders (who may or may not initially occupy formal leadership roles) in the ongoing and omnipresent task of inculcating culture. Someone who might never really "hear" the vision from you might pick it up easily from someone else.

Use the following seven checkpoints to create a mission that is easily understood, and that grabs people both mentally and emotionally. If you already have a mission, use these checks as tests, get feedback, and hit the drawing board as necessary. Now that you have an inspirational vision that is the emergent property of the repeated actions described in your mission, you're ready to tackle the third organizational function: capacity!

CHECK	6	**Our mission is action(s) done repeatedly**
CHECK	7	**Our mission brings about our vision**
CHECK	8	**Our mission explains WHO does WHAT for WHOM**
CHECK	9	**Our mission is clear, concise, and easily understood**
CHECK	10	**We measure our mission**
CHECK	11	**We ensure our mission lives in hearts and minds**
CHECK	12	**We ensure that mission moments are sacrosanct**

Figure 3.9: Checks for a well-designed mission

CHAPTER 4 ALIGN CAPACITY (C)

CHECK 1	Our vision depicts a desired future state
CHECK 2	Our vision is intrinsically motivating
CHECK 3	Our vision is short and simple
CHECK 4	We measure our vision
CHECK 5	We ensure our vision lives in hearts and minds
CHECK 6	Our mission is action(s) done repeatedly
CHECK 7	Our mission brings about our vision
CHECK 8	Our mission explains WHO does WHAT for WHOM
CHECK 9	Our mission is clear, concise, and easily understood
CHECK 10	We measure our mission
CHECK 11	We ensure our mission lives in hearts and minds
CHECK 12	We ensure that mission moments are sacrosanct
CHECK 13	**We build capacity in order to do our mission**
CHECK 14	**We build capacity through a system of systems**
CHECK 15	**We map capacity to understand and better design systems**
CHECK 16	**We use learning to expand our capacity**
CHECK 17	We harness the power of mental models
CHECK 18	We train people to think in order to learn
CHECK 19	We constantly evolve our mental models
CHECK 20	We create a culture of vision, mission, capacity, and learning

ALIGN CAPACITY (C)

There is nothing so useless as doing efficiently
that which should not be done at all.
—Peter Drucker

We should work on our process, not the outcome
of our processes.
—W. Edwards Deming

Now you know what you want the future to look like (vision), and the steps you need to take, repeatedly to get there (mission). Awesome. This is the stuff of exceptionally engaging off-site meetings. So, when you get back to the office, how are you going to get it done? What people do you need? What tools will they need? And how will you help them share and shift their mental models so that every day, every member of your team is doing your mission? (roadmaps, plans), procedural (policies, workflows), financial (models), and so on. It even includes people (hiring, human resources). In this chapter, we will help you think through how to tailor your organization's capacity to meet the specific needs of your mission.

We'll show you how to build a system of mission-critical systems, and we'll help you understand what all of these systems do. And while capacity is every bit as unsexy as we're making it sound, we promise, soon you'll be admiring its extremely practical dad bod.

Check #13: We Build Capacity to Do Our Mission

What is capacity? Capacity is a general term, used in disciplines from physics and mathematics to the military and ecology. Capacity is potential energy. Capacity is a state of preparedness or readiness to do something. But, more specifically, organizational capacity is the energy to do the mission. In other words, it is quite possible that you know exactly what your mission is and that you even have the opportunity to do your mission (i.e., you have a customer ready to be served), yet you do not have the capacity to actually serve them. That is why your organization needs to prepare itself by building capacity to do what it wants to repeatedly do (your mission).

Capacity—the form of the word that is synonymous with capability—denotes the ability or power to produce, perform, or deploy. People (and all other organisms) have capacity, objects have capacity, and organizations have capacity. But saying one has capacity immediately begs the question: the capacity for what? Capacity is made meaningful when tied to a purpose. Let's consider this both abstractly and in simple terms. The two containers in Figure 4.1 are similar in function and size and purpose (the capacity to hold liquid). But one structural difference leads one container to have less capacity than the other. The hole in one container means it has diminished capacity to achieve it's purpose and hold water (i.e., "do the mission").

Figure 4.1: Two similar structures with different capacity

Capacity Is a State of Readiness to Do Your Mission

A state of readiness to do your mission entirely depends on the capacity an organization develops. Motivation or desire to do something is not enough: you must build the capacity needed to accomplish your goals. Action of any kind requires capacity. Whenever you have something to *do* (mission), you need to also have the capacity to do it. This means that capacity isn't just a nice thing to consider—it is a universal function of all organisms and organizations. It is required, not optional. This relationship between action and capacity applies as much to physical objects and individuals as it does to organizations.

Let's look at an example. If you've ever prepared for a big talk, a big game, a big meeting, or a big test, you know that there's a moment when all the preparations are done and it's time to perform. Everything prior to that moment is capacity. After that moment is mission (i.e., the action). That's the reason the Boy Scout motto is "Be prepared." It is the reason Olympic athletes and musicians practice. Capacity is what you have in the tank when it's time to perform.[1]

Far too often, we are clear on what we want to do, but are less clear on all the things that need to be in place in order to do it. Think about a restaurant you dined at recently. Your experience was mostly informed by the overall level of service provided throughout your meal. What you don't see is the different types of capacity that were built to facilitate the moment your meal arrived. For example, the owner purchased all the ingredients for your food; the chef prepared the meal; another company delivered fresh linens; someone washed all the glasses; and each server, busser, chef, sommelier, maître d', and dishwasher received training. The aggregation of all these things—not just in the abstract, but as a shared mental model in the hearts and minds of the entire restaurant staff—is the restaurant's capacity, its readiness and ability to serve you. In other words, without meticulous attention to the range of capacity systems needed to do their mission of providing you with an exceptional experience, the restaurant would fail.

Figure 4.2: Successful mission moments depend upon capacity

This is true of all individuals and groups. You can't run on vision alone, you need to know the actions you need to repeatedly take (mission) to get you there. But you also need to know what capacity is required to do the mission.

You can build capacity in a lot of ways that don't help your business. So it becomes essential to ask yourself, "The capacity to do what?" to make sure that you are building not just any capacity, but the *right* capacity. In the same way that

your vision and mission need to be aligned, so too does your mission and capacity. So when we say that you need to build capacity, what we really mean is that you need to build a system of mission-critical systems. Then we can stay closer to the original purpose of these systems—to provide capacity to do the mission, which in turn achieves the vision.

The Things You Do Every Day Build Capacity

In a fictitious example, let's say our organization's vision is to "Eradicate Fleas Worldwide." To do this, our mission is to Evangelize, Educate, and Empower people to eradicate fleas. As part of the education element of our mission, we begin our efforts by offering training to disseminate these fundamental ideas to relevant audiences. The question we now face is, "What are the systems we have in place (or need to develop) to accomplish this task?" These individual systems, as seen in Figure 4.3, can begin with individual employees. In this image we see how an employee's daily tasks (like creating a brochure) can lead to increased capacity systems (by way of an existing training development resource) to do one part of the mission (educate people) to bring about the vision (to eradicate fleas worldwide).

Figure 4.3: A capacity map showing its contextualizing effect on employee daily tasks

This simple example shows how the things that employees do everyday should exist on a path through the organization's VMCL (blue line). The red lines indicates the global-level path that is created when there is throughput at the local-level from capacity to mission to vision. It also shows that something as mundane as designing and printing a brochure can be a capacity-building act (as long as it is aligned with the mission!) By planning ahead to build these mission-critical systems you can ensure that the moment when a customer needs a brochure, your salesperson will have one to hand them. That's an example (albeit a simple one) of organizational capacity playing out during a mission moment.

Capacity and Mission Must Be Aligned

When the linkage between capacity and mission is broken or "de-coupled" (i.e., when capacity does not directly serve the mission), systems (departments, teams, processes) can regress to a state in which their purpose is maintaining themselves rather than furthering the larger organizational mission. These systems can unknowingly adopt the implicit vision of being self-sustaining and do mission (repeated daily actions) that further that end state instead of furthering the organization's vision.

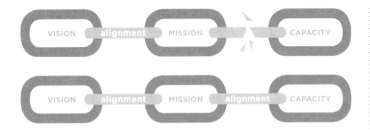

Figure 4.4: Mission and capacity: aligned versus unaligned

A system becomes bureaucratic when its purpose is de-coupled from the mission of the organization and therefore it has an alternative purpose for existing—which is often just to further its own existence. Although the term *bureaucracy* has alternative meanings in management science (some of them that don't have negative connotations) it is widely considered in the public usage to be negative. It usually refers to a company or system that is hindered by unnecessary red tape or inefficiencies. As we define it, bureaucracy—the de-coupling of capacital systems from the organization's mission—can be incredibly costly. One way to measure the broken link between mission and capacity is to identify and measure bureaucracy within an organization. At a multinational level, excess bureaucracy costs the 35 member countries of the Organisation for Economic Co-operation and Development (OECD) a total of 9 trillion dollars. For the United States, these costs amount to more than 3 trillion dollars in lost economic output, this amounts to around 17 percent of the U.S. GDP.[2]

Gary Hamel and Michele Zanini determined the excess costs of bureaucracy for a 2016 *Harvard Business Review* article through detailed economic analyses that found that if 15% of employees were re-deployed to focus on value-creation, mission-driven activities, they would each contribute an additional $141,000 in economic output per year. This increased productivity would significantly grow the U.S. GDP. In this new mental model, employees are re-assigned to value-creation tasks and are more likely to be satisfied with their work and more productive, thus producing more economic output.[3]

Many industries recognize the negative impact of bureaucracy on an organization's mission. For example, leaders in the pharmaceutical industry argue that the only way to reduce drug discovery costs and increase research and development (R&D) productivity is to disassemble excess bureaucracy. To start, as suggested by Roger Perlmutter, president of Merck Research Laboratories, companies would need to "scrape off the top five levels of management, including myself."[4] From a healthcare perspective, researchers have found that excess bureaucracy in the form of higher administrative costs often does not translate in better care for patients.[5] In other words, the existence of excessive administrative systems works against the primary mission of the organization. But is this model too simplistic? The cost of bureaucracy may vary depending on the industry or organization. A simplistic model to understand the cost of bureaucracy in for-profit organizations would be to look at the general and administrative expenses versus cost ratio. Although a portion of general and administrative expenses are necessary capacity systems that drive mission, they are often inflated. When assessing the expenses as a percentage of revenue over time, organizations should seek a fixed or declining ratio. This outcome would ensure that bureaucratic expenses are not inflating in comparison with revenue-generating activities, which are often more direct ways to accomplish mission. It is important to note the importance of many systems that *indirectly* contribute to our mission, such as human resources, purchasing, and so forth. These systems are necessary to maintain the organization's existence, and therefore, to the ability to do mission. Analyzing our organization's capacity to do mission must therefore include all systems that are directly or indirectly tied to mission. This helps us determine if there is, in fact, any inflation or redundancy in our system that can be streamlined for increased efficiencies.

Analyzing our organization's capacity to do mission must therefore include all systems that are directly or indirectly tied to mission.

The more important question to answer is: how closely are any systems (administrative or revenue-generating) tied to the mission? This is why it is so important to establish a clear and measureable mission, allowing us to determine the degree to which various systems contribute their capacity to the mission.

Think of a capacital system (a team, process, system, etc.)	How is each system providing capacity for mission?	What is your mission (or an element of your mission) and how is it measured?
Examples: • HR • Hiring process • The way we do meetings	We start meetings with our mission and its metrics to help ensure that the meeting content is framed by our mission	To increase user mapping activities measured by edits per day
Your turn:	Your turn:	Your turn:

Activity 4.1: Capacity-coupled-to-mission activity

There is also a large degree of path-dependence in organizational structure and practice so leaders in particular industries may invest in building specific capacities because they are normative and expected, rather than because they further the mission. However, recognizing that your organization is a complex adaptive system operating in a volatile, uncertain, complex, ambiguous environment requires flexible thinking rather than auto-adoption of "best practices" or latest trends. Therefore, visionary leadership hinges on seeing a future that others can't envision, standing in that future, and describing what you see. If your vision of the future is truly different, it's likely that the mission steps you take on a daily basis to get there will require the support of a new and different system of systems (capacity).

Aligning mission and capacity has a lot to do with how clear your mission is. To illustrate this, let's return to the example of restaurants, specifically farm-to-table restaurants.

Chef and restaurateur Alice Waters pioneered the farm-to-table movement. However, her original intention was never to start a movement. Instead, inspired by her travels in France, her mission was to open a restaurant that delivered high-quality, delicious, and flavorful food. This mission was in opposition to many restaurants around her in Northern California at the time, particularly fast-food restaurants that delivered food that was fast, cheap, and easy, without particular regard to quality. Waters opened her restaurant, Chez Panisse, in Berkeley, California in 1971[6] with the mission to serve meals focused on the best tastes and flavors.[7,8] Waters recognized that to carry out her mission she would have to build different capacities than most restaurants. Once she knew the mission, it was important to ask the all-important capacity question: what systems do I need in place to make it possible to deliver *the highest quality and best tasting meals*?

For Waters, it was all about the ingredients. Waters believed that to deliver on quality and taste, she would not be able to source nonorganic, commercially produced ingredients from distant farms (from which many restaurants, particularly those serving fast food, get their ingredients). Instead, she would need to source local, organic ingredients, that the Chez Panisse team believed tasted better than the commercial, nonorganic alternatives. Waters once explained in an interview:

"I know very well that in order to cook something that is really flavorful, you need to have ingredients that are grown in a place where they really thrive and so you're looking to the farmer to plant the right seeds in the right place and care for them, and know when to pick them."[9]

When Waters opened Chez Panisse, she could have made her life much easier by sourcing capacity from a food-service distributor like Sysco.[10] Distributors like Sysco are ready-made capacity for food establishments, because they coordinate food suppliers and producers. Additionally, because of their expansive capacity systems, large food distributors can often source any ingredient at any time of year, making menu options endless. If you want make a blueberry tart and it's not blueberry season, not to worry. Sysco has you covered and can source blueberries from locations around the world, allowing restaurants to have their mission-moments on demand.

Waters knew, however, that a distributor like Sysco could not provide the capacity she needed to meet her unique and innovative vision-mission. Her vision-mission required capacity not yet available in a pre-established system. Instead, she needed to build her own systems to carry-out her vision-mission.

Waters deeply understood that building the right capacity system drives mission. The chef and her team at Chez Panisse built critical systems from scratch. This included menus that change nightly at Chez Panisse because they are based on the availability of the best organic, seasonal and sustainable ingredients each day. Her suppliers needed to facilitate this.[11] In fact, Waters and her team built a network of local farmers, artisans, and producers to source the ingredients on the menus.[12] This process required an enormous level of effort.

Waters was a visionary leader, she saw a future that others couldn't envision, stood in that future, and worked tirelessly to describe and bring about what she saw. Farmers, like Paul Muller of Full Belly Farm in Northern California, remember Waters from the early days of Chez Panisse as the "wild woman who drove around in her truck looking for vegetables."[13] It is this kind of "in the trenches" work that is central to building new capacity that serves startup's, highly differentiated, disruptive, or innovative missions.

Waters's passionate commitment to her mission resulted in lasting changes in American food. Many credit Waters with encouraging the growth of organic agriculture in Northern California through her capacity-building efforts, which created more options for restaurants like hers to source local and organic ingredients.[14]

Once we begin to understand the necessary systems (things that a customer or client interacts with) to do our mission then we will likely need to ask:

What systems do I need in place to *support* those mission-critical systems?

And, of course, that likely will mean you need some second-order systems that are necessary to most organizations, whether you are building or managing a restaurant or a tech business. This includes things with which a customer or client may or may not interact, such as payroll, task management, administration, a customer relationship management (CRM) system, among others. Now that you've identified the systems you need to do your specific mission (not simply because some traditional model says you need them), you can start mapping and building these capacity systems. Later we will talk about measuring the health or influence of these systems, which is also an important aspect of ensuring mission-capacity alignment.

Try this: think through the flowchart in Figure 4.5 to determine if your capacity aligns with your mission.

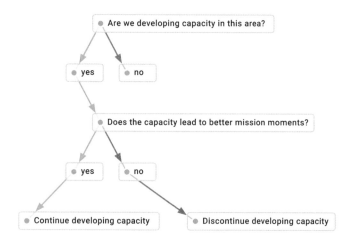

Figure 4.5: Couple capacity with mission

"The Purpose of a System Is What It Does."

We must sound a cautionary note on evaluating whether capacity and mission align. Systems and management scientist Stafford Beer developed an important and popular systems thinking heuristic known by the acronym POSIWID: "The purpose of a system is what it does." Beer regarded POSIWID as "bald fact" and a better starting point for understanding a system than a focus on designers' or users' intention or expectations.[15] When assessing alignment, we need to focus on what the system actually does rather than its ostensible, original, or ideal purpose (since these often do not match).

POSIWID has other important implications. It means that we need to think differently about how much control we really have over complex systems. Where capacity systems consist of many subsystems integrated into a system of systems, we want to look at them individually and collectively and ask:

• What is the system's stated (ostensible) purpose?
• What is the system's behavior?
• What does that behavior say about what the system's purpose is?
• Is there alignment between the actual and ostensible purpose?
• If not, what is the system's structure?
• How can we alter the structure to drive new behavior?[16]

In Activity 4.2, you can see the value of POSIWID thinking. It flips the system and its purpose on its head. Instead of looking at the results of a system as *problematic*, you look at the results of the system as *designed* or *by design*. The worse the result, the more clear the value of POSIWID thinking. Take, for example, a company that is bleeding cash: you might look at this as a problem (and of course it is), but for a moment consider that everything about that company—all of its internal systems—are actually really good at spending money. This flips the problem on its head. We can now look for processes, cultural morays, and other parts of the system that are good at burning cash. Recasting the system's purpose as POSIWID recasts the problem you are trying to solve.

Identify a system that you think is failing or isn't working well enough	Describe the specific results of the failure	Turn your description on its head with POSIWID*
Example: The U.S. education system	Too many disengaged kids	The U.S. education system is exceptionally well designed and good at its purpose of controlling and boring kids so that they disengage.
Example: Acme's software product	Too much churn	Acme's software product is extremely well designed and effective at its purpose of getting customers interested enough to sign up and then leave.
Your turn:	Your turn:	_____ is exceptionally well *entry from column 1 (system)* designed and good at its purpose of _____ . *entry from column 2 (results)*

Activity 4.2: POSIWID activity

Instead of the system being badly designed to serve a good outcome, it is brilliantly designed at bringing about a bad outcome.

One way to determine whether a system stated purpose is also its actual purpose (which should be mission) is to measure or assess its effectiveness.

Remember what Einstein said: "Not everything that is measured matters and not everything that can be measured, matters." Don't measure everything about a system, measure what matters. What matters in capacity systems? This is simple: how much capacity do they produce to do your mission? That's it. That's all that matters in these systems. Do they contribute to making your mission happen? As such, capacity assessment is a mission-critical system within all organizations.

Capturing, measuring, interpreting, and using data is a critical part of organizational life and a necessary focus of leadership. A dashboard is a metaphorical (or actual as realized through one of many cloud-based platforms) snapshot of the important data or metrics of your organization. Some of the more important metrics on your dashboard should pertain to mission. You need measures—indicators—of your capability to do your mission.

As an uncommitted student in his early 20s at the University of Oregon, Derek was swept up in the regional conflict either endearingly or pejoratively (depending on which side you were on) represented by the spotted owl. Loggers and the logging industry were pitted against environmentalists and (literally) tree huggers. One side wanted the industry jobs and natural resources that resulted from clear cutting the old growth of Oregon's lush forests, while the other side wanted the ecological and recreational conservation of those same lush forests. The spotted owl really wasn't the issue, but it was an *indicator species*. Scientists had determined that the size of the spotted owl population was an indicator of the larger health of the forest ecosystem. By maintaining an ongoing count of owls in the forest, scientists were measuring its health. Thus was born the "poster owl" for a movement to protect the forests.

What matters in capacity systems? This is simple: how much capacity do they produce to do your mission? That's it. That's all that matters in these systems. Do they contribute to making your mission happen?

There are countless "indicator species" in nature and in business and society—variables that tell us something about the big picture. These indicators are feedback from the real world. They're easier to count than, say, the qualitative health of a forest ecosystem. Lichen, for example, only grows in areas where the air quality is high. You won't often find lichen in cities. If lichens are in decline, the real world is giving you feedback not merely about lichens but about the air quality of the city itself.[17, 18]

One of the keys to monitoring capacity is to find the right "indicator species" to help you quickly measure the health of your systems, which is determined by a single outcome: whether systems are providing capacity for you to do your mission. Of course, there are often different indicators for each system, as well as the system of systems as a whole. But before you go on a hunt for low-hanging indicators, remember that you must find a way to *measure what matters*. We are awash in information. But one of the keenest insights from the field of research methodology is "just because you can [collect data] doesn't mean you should." Despite the current fixation with big data, having a lot of data isn't in itself important. Having the right data is important. Measure what matters.

Here's another way in which measurement is deceptively tricky. Often the ability to *quantitatively* measure something comes from the capacity to *qualitatively* understand it. This means that simply counting the things you can count isn't enough.

Better to understand the things you want to measure (in science this is called *construct validity*) and learn, over time, to measure them.

Let's examine, for example, customer satisfaction. What is customer satisfaction? You might say that the degree to which folks continue to buy your product is a good indicator of customer satisfaction. Yet we've continued to subscribe to the cable company's service for our home for years. However, every time we see that there's an emerging product on the horizon that might replace our dependence on cable, we get giddy. The second that product is viable, we'll toss cable like a used Kleenex. Until then, we'll continue our subscription, but are we really satisfied? A better but somewhat more difficult measurement to assess is how much we rave about a particular company, service, or product.

The point is to think of metrics as measurements that are ever evolving to capture reality. And, most important, remember that ability to understand a thing qualitatively *must* precede attempts to measure it quantitatively. You have to figure out which indicator you need to be assessing and how might you go about measuring it.

Check #14: We Build Capacity Through a System of Systems

Alignment Entails Creating a System of Systems

Not only must capacity be aligned with mission (i.e., provide the ability to do the mission), it must also be a *system of systems* rather than just a bunch of systems. Before tackling that idea, let's start more simply. Much of your organization's capacity derives from various systems. So what are systems? A dictionary definition of system is "an assemblage or combination of things or parts forming a complex or unitary whole."[19] For our purposes, systems are the mechanism for building and holding capacity. A system might be

- A structural system (a device, team, division, or department)
- A systemic process (a series of steps or dynamical operations)
- A conceptual system (a method, axiom, or philosophy)
- A mixed system (e.g., an amalgam of the above)

Let's list some all-too-familiar examples. Management theorist Henri Fayol described "six essential functions of all industrial enterprise, irrespective of the type of organization."[20]

They were

1. Technical activities (production, manufacture, adaptation)
2. Commercial activities (buying, selling, exchange)
3. Financial activities (search for and optimum use of capital)
4. Security activities (protection of property and persons)
4. Accounting activities (stocktaking, balance sheet, costs, statistics)
5. Managerial activities (planning, organization, command, coordination, control)

Fayol's list (from 1916!) widely influenced the common departmental structures (or systems) we see in organizations today, including engineering, research and development, purchasing, sales and marketing, human resources, accounting, and finance. Although we tend to think of these as departments or divisions, we are better served to think of them as systems. The term *department* is derived from the 18th-century Old French *departement*, which is rooted in an old Latin verb meaning to "separate from" or "divide".[21] This is of course counter to what we want in a system of systems (see below). As a result, we prefer the terms *systems* and *subsystems*.

Each system (or department) has a particular function. The question you must ask yourself is, "What are the mission-critical systems I need in order to do my mission?" Regardless, any complex organization will be characterized by multiple systems—you want these systems to be part of a larger system (this is an ongoing leadership task of coordination and alignment). For simplification purposes, we might differentiate first-order systems from second-order systems. First-order systems (say, sales and marketing) provide capacity that is directly related to the mission, whereas second-order systems (such as payroll) are required for the mission, but less directly related to it.

The key to developing mission-aligned capacity is not merely to create a bunch of systems but to design a system of systems. As illustrated in Figure 4.6, that system of systems needs to be *entirely* focused on your mission. That is, you must not merely develop various types of organizational capacity to do *stuff*, but exclusively to do your *mission*. Capacity manifests itself in the form of myriad systems—from formal ones such as organizational structure and policy and shipping and receiving to informal ones like social networks, motivation, and office humor.

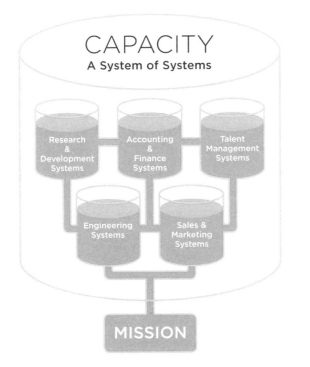
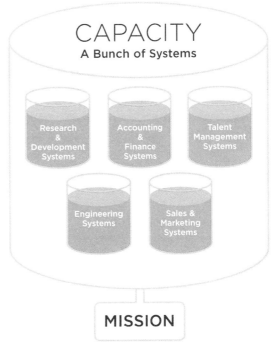

Figure 4.6: A system of systems versus a bunch of systems

Making sure you have the right systems and that you not only conceptually understand but also put formal and physical (in terms of support, functions or resources) capacity into ensuring their interrelationships will inoculate your organization from a diffracted or siloed capacity. Which mission-critical systems are the right ones? How do you begin mapping these systems to ensure they become a systems of systems rather than a bunch of systems? Let's explore this a bit more.

The key to developing mission-aligned capacity is not merely to create a bunch of systems but to design a system of systems.

How Do I Know Which Systems Are Mission-Critical Systems?

The capacital systems that are mission-critical to your organization are highly dependent on your organization's mission. As we saw in the example of chef and restaurateur Alice Waters, her unique mission required her to create some very specific homegrown capacital systems. At the same time, many organizations share a common set of mission-critical systems based on their developmental period or size. For example, if you're a tech startup it is often the case that your first two mission-critical systems are engineering and sales; you have to build something and you have to sell it. Thoughtful CEOs, like Mark Benioff of Salesforce, advocate adding a talent acquisition system early on; the thought being that who you get on the team is mission-critical. As your company grows, new capacities are needed. But make sure that they are needed either (1) to build capacity directly for the mission (first-order, or mission-critical, systems), or (2) to provide capacity for other mission critical systems (second-order systems). For these second-order systems, there should be a direct through line that connects their function to mission-critical systems and then to mission and vision.

There are many capacital systems you may need to get the job done and not all of these systems are at the departmental scale (i.e., sales engineering, human resources, marketing, etc). In our work with organizations, folks usually have a good handle on the departmental level systems, but often ask us about smaller-scale systems or meta-level systems (systems that cut across systems). They often ask us about core values, workflows, and even smaller systems like how to run meetings or how to develop better communication—these, too, are systems that may need to be considered. Some of these systems are just new ways to think through how you do things (workflows such as Kanban or Agile, design thinking, or objectives and key results). Others are cross-cutting systems, such as new ways to think about how teams will run more effective meetings or whether Power-Point will be banned. Then there are other cultural or conceptual systems, such as core values or principles. Below we take you through a few such examples to give you an idea of how they fit into building your capacity to do your mission.

Systems of Capacity: Workflows, OKRs, and Other Processes

If your vision is aligned with your mission and your mission is aligned with your capacity systems, as you go into deeper detail of all the subsystems of capacity, you'll eventually reach the specific things people are doing (tasks or to-do lists) on any given day. For obvious reasons, all of the specific daily tasks that people in the organization are doing should be aligned with the long-term vision of the organization (as we saw in the case of the employee who developed an educational flea brochure above).

We might think of a to-do list or task list as the most basic tool for capacity building—a task list or task management system helps people to see, share, and update what they are doing each day, and there are countless apps and cloud-based software (with varying degrees of complexity) available. Moving upward from this basal level, you might use a specific method or tool for managing quarterly goals such as objectives and key results (OKR), which originated at Intel and was popularized by Google. Today, OKR has become so popular as to have spawned a micro-industry of cloud applications for implementing OKR (Perdoo, 7Geese, BetterWorks, etc.). The popularity of management by OKR is partly due to its simplicity and partly by the success of its more prominent corporate users. OKR can be quite simple. Table 4.1 describes objectives and some measurable key results for two focus areas (sales and customer success).

Objective	Key Results
Sales[22]	
Accelerate recurring revenue growth this quarter	• Deliver $2M in subscription revenues • Increase monthly revenue / subscriber to $65 • Hire 3 new inside sales people
Expand revenue footprint in Asia	• Hire 10 channel partners in key geographies • Drive new compensation plan for Asia sales team • Deliver 5 compelling region-specific success stories
Customer Success	
Deliver amazing customer support experience	• Implement new customer support software • Average problem resolution time < 24 hours • Customer sat survey scores of > 4
Significant revenue increase per customer	• Implement new compensation model for customer support • Retrain team on upsell of new products • Revenue per customer increases by 20% • Increase customer retention to 95%

Table 4.1: Examples of OKR

The purpose of OKR is to align the work of individuals, teams, and the organization as a whole with a common purpose. That purpose is your mission, which (done repeatedly) will bring about your vision. We will review what it looks like to manage capacity through the OKR process, but there are many other capacity-building tools and models both for capacity writ large and for building capacity in specialized areas.

Capacity is not the same as OKR. OKR is a tool for building capacity. Capacity is just a universal and timeless function for getting things done. Your organization may choose or not choose to use OKR as a tool, but it simply cannot ignore the function of capacity as a necessary ingredient to your success. Without the capacity to act, there is no action.

Regardless of whether you use task management or OKR systems, or both, the more important goal is that when an employee is doing something (even a relatively small or mundane task, or something larger like a quarterly objective) he or she should at least conceptually be able to see the path between the time and resources allocated to that task or objective and the capacity systems, mission, and vision of the organization. In Figure 4.7 path (red arrows) shows the general path (for example) from tasks to capacity, mission, and eventually vision.

In path (blue arrows) you see a more detailed path from a specific task to a second-order subsystem of capacity that supports a first-order subsystem in carrying out the repeatable mission and in turn brings about the vision.

We are not advocating per se that the paths shown in Figure 4.7 are formal or even explicit, but merely that any employee of an organization should be occasionally reflective about how the things they are doing matter to the larger mission and vision of the organization. This deep understanding of the importance of one's work, its relevance, and connection to something larger and more important than the task itself is crucial for authentic engagement, intrinsic motivation, and long-term sustainability factors such as attrition.

Figure 4.7: From to-do list to done vision

Core Values: A System of Capacity

What are core values, and why does every company feel compelled to create and publicize them?[23] The growing emphasis on organizational culture has likely fueled this trend: many CEOs equate culture with values. For example, a *Harvard Business Review* piece reads: "*Core values* are the deeply ingrained principles that guide all of a company's actions; they serve as its cultural cornerstones."[24] Another way to think of a company's "deeply ingrained principles" is the mental models that all members share. In reality, however, what companies subsume under the term *values* is remarkably diverse and demonstrates inconsistent usage of the word. For example, there is frequent semantic confusion between a company's vision, their values, and their mission.

Although *values* and *culture* are often used synonymously, values are best understood as part of capacity. Values should enable (provide capacity for) an organization to achieve its vision. This definition of values helps explain why:

> Core values are what support the vision, shape the culture and reflect what the company values...Many companies focus mostly on the technical competencies but often forget what are the underlying competencies that make their companies run smoothly—core values.[25]

Therefore, while we are agnostic as to whether organizations should create value statements, we suggest that they should be conceptualized as organizational capacity. Doing so will ensure that your values align with (help achieve) your vision.

Although values and culture are often used synonymously, values are best understood as part of capacity. Values should enable an organization to achieve its vision.

This means all your values should align with your mission and vision. Your VMCL mental models—the cornerstone of your culture—should be relatively enduring. There are other types of mental models you might use that aren't core, but may also persist, provided they align with your VMCL. For example, many companies use *The Four Agreements*[26] as a mental model to help people manage interpersonal relationships (an aspect of capacity). Other mental models might be built around incentives or mascots. For example, REI (an outdoor equipment retailer) selects outdoors-oriented employees who live the REI culture.[27] Employees have the opportunity to win equipment by submitting "challenge grants" proposing challenging outdoor adventures.[28]

Some mental models are more subject to change as the organization evolves. For example, your culture might prescribe how meetings are run (e.g., Amazon and the US Military have eschewed PowerPoint [29]), how feedback is given, or other customs governing day-to-day operations.

So let's review our definition of culture and our understanding of its purpose:

- Culture is shared mental models.
- Organizational culture is constituted by the mental models shared by an organization's members.
- Culture is the mechanism to purposefully leverage the natural functions of any organization.

Leaders often say their most valuable weapon is their people. We disagree. People in and of themselves aren't that powerful, especially if they are bickering, working at cross purposes, or ignoring one another. People who share common mental models (i.e., culture) are powerful.

A Better Meetings System

Amazon re-imagined the way companies traditionally hold meetings. According to Jeff Bezos:

> The traditional kind of corporate meeting starts with a presentation. Somebody gets up in front of the room and presents with a powerpoint presentation, some type of slide show. In our view you get very little information, you get bullet points. This is easy for the presenter, but difficult for the audience.[30]

Jeff Bezos determined that meetings structured around PowerPoint didn't provide the necessary capacity to support the mission (or repeated actions) of the organization. So instead, Jeff Bezos developed a narrative process (i.e., a new capacital system), to meet the needs of their organization.

This process, still used by the company, structures meetings around a 4-page to 6-page, evidence-based, narrative memo. These memos are prepared meticulously by teams within the organization prior to each meeting. At the meeting, the first 20 minutes of the meeting are devoted to reading the document, then the group discusses (and sometimes debates) the content of the memo by diligently questioning the presenting team. The benefits of this process are two-fold. First, it requires the team involved to have a deep understanding of the issue, and its context.[31]

Also, perhaps more important, it ensures that everyone in the meeting has the same mental model of the issue at hand.

This process scales how organizations can share information within and between capacital systems, and make decisions as informed by these capacities.

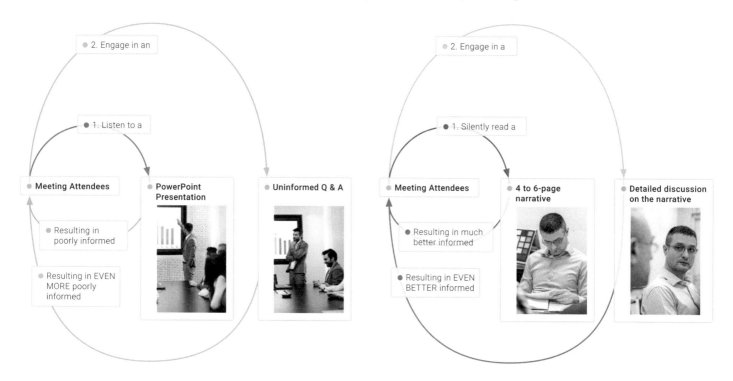

Figure 4.8: Traditional meetings versus Bezos's narrative meetings

Check #15: We map capacity in order to understand and better design these systems

Your capacity is typically constituted by an amalgam of systems and processes that is too complex to accurately capture and understand. Despite the complexity of organizational capacity, you can develop mental models that capture a relatively good approximation of what these systems are doing. You then test the veracity, validity, and reliability of these mental models against reality, and use the feedback to develop better models. This is required so you can tweak the simple rules of the system and the actions of the agents working within it.

It is nearly impossible to improve your capacity unless you model its constituent pieces. This enables us to discern the behavior of all systems and see if they are in line with the mission. When it comes to depicting and analyzing a system, a precise visual illustration trumps an abundance of words. Building a map will help you assess whether and how each system increases your ability, either directly or indirectly, to perform the repeated actions (i.e., mission) necessary to bring about your vision. It is also quite useful (including for allocating time, effort, and other resources) to establish some measurement of capacity (and eventually metrics) for each system in your organization. Adding measurements to systems and subsystems in your capacity map allows you to add capacital metrics to your organizational dashboard along with your vision (V) and mission (M) metrics.

Remember that we are dealing with mental models of your organization's capacity systems. As such, maps of your capacity are ever-evolving, living, "evergreen" documents, so these maps should be a snapshot based on the evolving reality on the ground. As the reality changes, so too should your map. Although one individual or a small team may create the original map of the organization's capacity, in the long run it is ideally informed by the perspectives of multiple individuals who occupy different roles within your organization.

Capacity Maps (CapMaps)

A map showing a system of systems that serves to further mission and, in turn, vision is a great first step in building a shared mental model (culture) of the importance and purpose of capacity in your organization. There are a variety of ways in which this can be done.

A capacity map can provide a very general overview of systems, or it can depict in intricate detail and from multiple perspectives the capacity of your systems. Different maps are useful for different purposes, organizational types, and audiences. For example, if you are a new organization without much existing structure or complexity, it may suffice to create a very general CapMap to get everyone on the same page.

But there are many other types including, "deep-dive" maps that locate an individual or team with respect to systems and subsystems; maps that link task management methods, such as OKR; maps that measure capacity (attach metrics to systems); and maps that contain a mix of structural and strategic/conceptual systems.

A map showing a system of systems that serves to further mission and in turn vision is a great first step in building a shared mental model (culture) of the importance and purpose of capacity in your organization.

While you have numerous choices to make about structure, purpose, design, and format, the most important thing about a CapMap is that you have one. The way you organize the systems in your organization is up to you. For example, you might want to conceptualize your capacity systems as common departmental functions: engineering, research and development, purchasing, sales and marketing, human resources, accounting and finance. So, the simplest form of CapMap would look something like Figure 4.9.

Figure 4.9: General overview (100,000-foot) CapMap of traditional systems

Of course, we could think more deeply about these systems and break them down further into related parts or challenge the distinctions between and among them. For example, "human resources" is a distinction that reminds us of the flawed traditional model in which humans are treated as utilizable resources. If we do not want to reinforce this notion this system function might be called, "attract and sustain talent" and the system might be called "talent" for short. We might want to separate marketing and sales or combine them, or think of R&D as a natural extension of an engineering department that uses short-cycle feedback loop methods, such as Sprints and Lean and Agile development.

Whether we are creating a new organization or reinventing an established one, we may want to throw out many of these traditional systems and start anew—this time with the end in mind. This means we start with the mission and ask ourselves what systems are necessary. For example, say our mission was to "Evangelize, Educate, and Empower," and we wanted to think about all the functions and systems we needed to do such a mission repeatedly. We might distinguish between first-order systems (those that are directly critical to the mission, such as sales and marketing or training) and second-order systems (those that are indirectly necessary for the mission, such as finance and accounting). Then our CapMap might look like Figure 4.10.

Figure 4.10: CapMap of modern systems
(first- and second-order)

As a leader, you must ensure that your employees have a shared understanding of capacity in your organization, not to mention their role in the mission and hence contribution to the vision. These things—mission, vision, and capacity (and learning)—are all inextricably related. If capacity seems banal, it's because you're failing to appreciate how it connects to mission and vision. Nothing helps build a shared mental model of capacity (and increase individual ownership in it) than a "you are here" CapMap.

A "You Are Here!" Map for Every Employee

Once they have created a 100,000-foot, big-picture CapMap, most organizations will want to dive deeper to capture the nuances of systems and subsystems. Leaders need to locate members of the system in relation to subsystems, processes, and/or tasks. This step is not unlike making a mall map that allows every member of your organization to know "You are here."

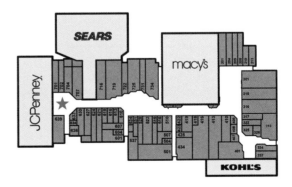

Figure 4.11: CapMaps can indicate "You Are Here"

Except instead of a map that shows a single person/location (say, Jim at Cinnabon), an organizational CapMap will show every employee where they are relative to the mission (which might mean "residing" in multiple systems).

A well-done CapMap will help every employee understand how their daily work either indirectly or directly supports the mission and, in turn, the vision. This has significant and lasting effects on the many factors shown to increase motivation. One way to do this is to give each leader of a system (let's call them each VP, for short) the task of building out the CapMap with details of their specific system. Each VP needs to break down the system (division, department, or similar) he or she oversees into subsystems, noting and defining relationships between and among systems (and their parts), and providing metrics on how much capacity is generated to do mission by each system whenever possible.

CapMaps Are Evergreen and Evolving

Creating a capacity map is the most efficient and effective way we know to create shared mental models of capacity (i.e., to enculturate capacity). Whether you choose to stop with an broad overview of your capacity or map your systems in a multitude of detailed ways, creating a CapMap is only the first step. You must ensure that this mental model of capacity systems and their link to mission is shared widely across the organization.

Again, we don't mean you should "share" them in the sense of sending an email, such as:

All Staff,

Please see our organizational CapMap attached:
http://www.acmecorp.com/OrgCapMap/

Thanks,

The Management

An alternative would be to use a general CapMap as a cultural icon (think large wall cling) that gives everyone a big picture view of the organization's mission-critical systems. It is of great importance that every member of your organization should be able to identify where they "live" in the CapMap and therefore how they contribute to mission (even if their contribution is indirect). They need to see it on a map and build a model of their contribution.

Sharing *information* is often of limited utility: sharing *meaning* is invaluable. This requires that people build shared understanding of and endorsement for capacity. They may need to unlearn or modify old mental models before learning new ones; this culture-building is an act of organizational and individual *learning*.

We cover learning in greater depth in the next chapter, but let's say that one day your VP of Talent comes in and says she just read an article titled, "How Uber got into this human resources mess" and it made her rethink your talent system. Your VP tells you that Uber made the mistake of focusing entirely on talent at the origin of the company and reads you an excerpt from the article.

> It's most glaring overall problems seems to center on how the human resources role was conceived at Uber by its brash and commanding leader Kalanick. The issue: he felt the function of HR at Uber was largely to recruit talent and also efficiently let go of personnel when needed, according to sources.[32]

Sharing *information* is often of limited utility: sharing *meaning* is invaluable. This requires that people build shared understanding of and endorsement for capacity.

Your VP of Talent doesn't want to make the same mistake and wants to change the name of her system to Human Talent and Behavior. You agree and you change the organization's CapMap. But your organization didn't have the conversation and insights that you and your VP of Human Talent and Behavior (her new title) just had. That awareness and the meaning of the distinction between "Talent" and "Human Talent and Behavior" needs to be made more explicit throughout the organization. CapMaps are mental models of your capacity, continuously updated based on feedback from the environment in order to better approximate the reality of your organization.

Burn the Neurons to Build Your CapMap in Five Easy Steps

Building a functional skeleton for a CapMap is easy. We recommend these five steps. As you learn new things each day, you can add some meat to the bones of your CapMap. The activity that follows is what we call a "draw this, say this" activity. At first you might decide to simply read through the activity, and not actually draw it or say it out loud. That's okay. We don't want folks on the train to think you're talking to yourself. But what we know about the brain is that it is very adept at learning new things. What we are showing you might not be the way you normally do things, so to learn it you'll have to fight against the neurons you've already built. In order to do this, a little neurolinguistic programming can help. By drawing it out and saying it out loud, we think you'll get much more out of it. Up to you.

Activity 4.3: "Draw this, say this" for capacity mapping

Step #1: The first step is to burn those neurons by drawing the following simple diagram and then saying the words that describe it: **Draw this:**

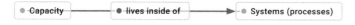

Say this: "My organization's capacity lives inside of the systems, or processes, of my organization."

Step #2: Draw this:

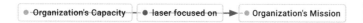

Say this: "My organization's capacity has to be laser-focused on my organization's mission."

Step #3: In this third step when you do the drawing, sketch out a few of your mission-critical systems (the ones in the drawing are generic)... **Draw this:**

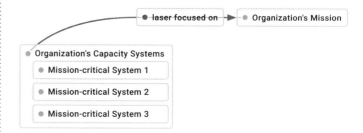

Say this: "My organization's capacity is a system that is made up of a bunch of mission-critical systems."

Activity 4.3: "Draw this, say this" for capacity mapping

Step #4: Draw this:

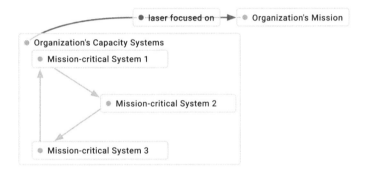

Say this: "It is super important that my mission-critical subsystems work as a system that is focused on my organization's mission, so I need to look at how these subsystems of capacity are interrelated. This will avoid silos forming in my organization, as well as ensuring that we build one system of systems rather than a bunch of systems."

Step #5: Draw this:

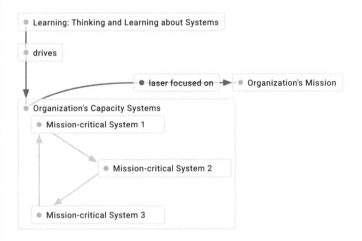

Say this: "Now that I've built my skeleton CapMap, I need to understand that the best way to understand and design those systems is to think and learn about them. Learning drives capacity which drives mission which drives vision."

Check #16: We Use Learning to Expand Our Capacity

Build a Culture of Learning by Capacity Hacking

As a leader, you want to build into your culture an appreciation of and proclivity for constant improvement—tweaking processes, reordering steps, imagining alternative mechanisms, and so forth—to improve them because it brings joy to you to make things better. Learning (which we will go into in depth in the next chapter) is the engine and the driver of capacity. A learning culture is a hacking culture. A culture that never accepts existing systems just because "that's how we've always done it." A learning, hacking culture is a culture that knows things can always be better, more efficient, more elegant… more beautiful! Can a system, process, workflow,

concept, or capacity really be more aesthetically pleasing? More elegant? More beautiful? You bet it can!

Hackathons have an attitude that is entrepreneurial and communal yet competitive and fun. You can demonstrate this orientation to capacity, reward innovations in process and system design, and celebrate success. Think Taylor without the stopwatch, but with a great sense of fun. We'll illustrate with a simple example.

Laura and Derek live on the edge of town in the country. They somehow came to have four dogs, and feeding them was always a production. During the years that their kids fed the dogs, the process and its outcome were variable and wildly inefficient. The dogs eventually got fed, but it was a tedious, time-consuming, mess-generating chore. When the dog-feeding fell to the adults, Laura wisely delegated it to Derek.

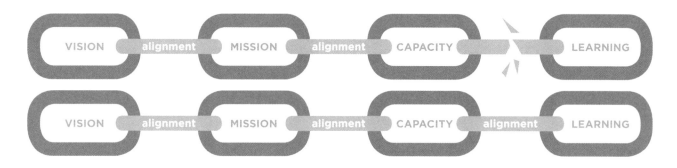

Figure 4.12: Make sure your learning is focused on capacity building or there will be no capacity building.

Figure 4.13: The rabble is getting restless... hacking systems to increase their capacity

In the first two weeks of feeding the dogs (two 130-pound Bernese Mountain Dogs and two obsessive-compulsive Australian Cattle Dogs), Derek reflected on the job and looked for inefficiencies. He broke down the process like any good Taylorian would. But as a systems thinker, Derek was also taking multiple factors into account, including his empathy and care for the dogs.

Derek noticed that the dogs would sort of bully one another and some would end up eating more and those who got less would spend more time begging for scraps throughout the day. He also saw that the big Berners have very large noses and relatively small bowls. Comically, their noses eclipse their food from sight and the small bowls cause the food to constantly overflow onto the floor, creating micro-stains that even avid dog licking can't remove. The nose-to-bowl size discrepancy also causes the dogs to push the stainless steel dishes across the floor to get at the food, generating a chorus of steel-on-tile screeching.

Reflecting on the feeding process, Derek noticed significant wasted walking time, as the bowls, the food, the feeding area, the water, and the scoop were all literally in different places. The water and food bowls (eight in total) were not stackable and hence hard to carry all at once (not to mention they took up an inordinate amount of space). After observing his own behavior and the daily feeding frenzy for a few days, Derek saw changes that could be made to the system.

• Move the food bin to a better location and tie a scoop to it.
• Purchase eight large stackable bowls with sticky-grip bottoms.
• Devise an order of operations and placement of bowls that decreased the infighting.

In doing this, he cut the time it takes to feed the furries by one-third, with less mess, less cleanup, less cacophony, and no conflict. The new system provides capacity to efficiently do the twice-daily feedings. Building that capacity required observing and learning and systems analysis.

The point here is that there's a certain joy in observing processes and the reflection and analysis that leads to efficiency gains by changing the way a system is structured. This holds whether one is feeding a dog, answering work emails, processing a personal to-do list, or managing the complex processes involved on a factory floor or in a brainstorming session. You need to make sure that improving capacity is everyone's job, and that it is fun and rewarded. Find ways to tap intrinsic and extrinsic motivations for everyone to become a capacity hacker.

You'll know you've failed to enculturate capacity if it is viewed as the exclusive domain of executives.

The capacity of your organization is tied to the capacities of its individuals. This means that building a culture of capacity means attracting and developing a cadre of folks who get excited about constantly learning, observing, thinking, paying attention to all the things around them, and making things better. Not just any things, but the systems that enable you to do the mission better and faster. Building capacity is never finished. It is a 24/7 constant improvement process.

Building a culture of capacity means attracting and developing a cadre of folks who get excited about constantly learning, observing, thinking, paying attention to all the things around them, and making things better.

CHECK	13	**We build capacity in order to do our mission**
CHECK	14	**We build capacity through a system of systems**
CHECK	15	**We map capacity to understand and better design systems**
CHECK	16	**We use learning to expand our capacity**

Figure 4.14: Checks for developing organizational capacity

The checkpoints above will help you to understand capacity and how it must function. While discussing capacity has taken us into the minutiae (systems, processes, details) of the organization, it's worth reiterating the big picture of capacity.

- Leadership means burning new neuronal pathways based on the idea that *everything we do must serve the mission.*
- The closest we can come to understanding capacity is through careful observation to discern the type of capability produced by every system in our organization. Then we must map it before we try to change it.

- We need to build and share and constantly evolve our mental models of capacity.
- Organizational capacity should be an agent-based (or crowd-sourced) affair—not a shared duty, but a fun and creative process we can all (always) undertake.

Of course, as with all organizational functions, capacity is also closely linked to learning. Learning—individual and organizational—is the topic of the next chapter.

CHAPTER 5 LOVE LEARNING (L)

CHECK	1	Our vision depicts a desired future state
CHECK	2	Our vision is intrinsically motivating
CHECK	3	Our vision is short and simple
CHECK	4	We measure our vision
CHECK	5	We ensure our vision lives in hearts and minds
CHECK	6	Our mission is action(s) done repeatedly
CHECK	7	Our mission brings about our vision
CHECK	8	Our mission explains WHO does WHAT for WHOM
CHECK	9	Our mission is clear, concise, and easily understood
CHECK	10	We measure our mission
CHECK	11	We ensure our mission lives in hearts and minds
CHECK	12	We ensure that mission moments are sacrosanct
CHECK	13	We build capacity in order to do our mission
CHECK	14	We build capacity through a system of systems
CHECK	15	We map capacity to understand and better design systems
CHECK	16	We use learning to expand our capacity
CHECK	17	**We harness the power of mental models**
CHECK	18	**We train people to think in order to learn**
CHECK	19	**We constantly evolve our mental models**
CHECK	20	We create a culture of vision, mission, capacity, and learning

LOVE LEARNING (L)

We now accept the fact that learning is a lifelong process of keeping abreast of change. And the most pressing task is to teach people how to learn.
—Peter Drucker

Tell me and I forget.
Teach me and I may remember.
Involve me and I learn.
—Benjamin Franklin

The success of any organization depends on its ability to learn: to adapt to feedback from the environment and thrive in the face of change. If you don't know what your vision is, or if you want to measure an aspect of your vision but don't know how, you need to learn. If you have a great mission but something is missing, or your customers are not doing what you anticipate, you need to learn. If your capacity systems aren't working the way you want them to, you need to learn. If you want to streamline a process to make it more efficient, or if your talent isn't motivated, self-directed, creative, innovative, committed, engaged, emotionally intelligent, or lacks any other skill or quality you need, you need to learn. Everyone in the organization will need to learn in order to build culture around your inspiring vision, your actionable mission, or your mission-critical system of systems (capacity).

We need to think about learning anew. We need to unlearn what it means to train employees— what training looks like and what its end goal is. The most important information you will ever impart to your fellow organization members is how to think and how to learn. This is because thinking drives learning and learning drives capacity, which makes mission possible and, in turn, brings about vision. But it all starts with building a culture that facilitates learning, adaptation, risk-taking, collaboration, and other qualities and activities critical to organizational learning.

So where do you start? How might you capture the complexity of your organization in order to facilitate this learning? Our research has spanned numerous fields of inquiry—from network and complexity theory; to systems thinking, human cognition, visual and tactile processing, and metacognition; to the learning sciences and organizational learning; and from science and technology studies to the study of knowledge itself (epistemology). Over the past 20 years, we have discovered that the act of *visually mapping one's ideas* is one of the single most effective ways to improve our understanding of complex systems. It is also one of the best methods for sharing ideas in a way that leads to two or more people constructing the same mental model. We could fill a whole book with the reasons why using your hands to move little shapes around a page increases understanding, clarity, and effectiveness in all domains. But here's just one: There are more neurons linking your brain to your eyes and your hands than to any other body parts.[1]

Early on, we started our visual mapping with simple shapes on paper or blackboards, then on larger sheets of paper and whiteboards. Over time, our research pointed to the obvious use of technology to facilitate the creation of these visual knowledge representations (maps). For years, folks would take snapshots with their cameras, and later with their phones, and then email or text them to their colleagues. Although effective, these fixed images lacked the capacity to be collaborative at a distance or to adapt and evolve. Interactive technology can solve these problems. But technology also makes something else possible—the canvas (the virtual whiteboard, if you will) can speak to you in a way that its analog cousin cannot. The canvas can provide better cognitive structures to help you build better ideas[2] to begin with, but it can also make suggestions that will further improve your analysis of systems that are important to you. In addition, there are many technological accoutrements—such as artificial intelligence, machine learning, natural language processing, and big data—that can be added to these suggestions to prompt the mapper to outthink, outdo, and outlast.

Building a culture of capacity means attracting and developing a cadre of folks who get excited about constantly learning, observing, thinking, paying attention to all the things around them, and making things better.

In order for your organization to truly excel at learning, you will need to help individual employees excel at thinking. That involves thinking critically about how you think— scientists call this *metacognition*. Research studies show that metacognition "increases success in all domains"[3] not just in analytical and scientific forms of thinking, but also in creativity and innovation, systems thinking or complex cognition, and even prosocial and emotional intelligence.

Throughout the course of this chapter, you will build and optimize a learning organization. To create a learning organization, you will need to check three things off your list:

• Check #17: We harness the power of mental models
• Check #18: We train people to think in order to learn
• Check #19: We constantly evolve our mental models

You will develop a practical understanding of how to create a team of continuous learners— who build, share, and evolve mental models—to constantly improve your organization's capacity to more effectively and efficiently do the mission and achieve the vision.

Check #17: We Harness the Power of Mental Models

An organization has to learn to survive. But in order for an organization to learn, its people have to learn. And in order for people to learn, they need to think. So, how do people think anyway? How do we think smarter? And why does it matter?

Most of the organizational problems we face result from the difference between how we *think* organizations work and how they *actually* work. The real world works in systems—complex networks of many interacting variables. *Systems thinking* attempts to better align how we think with how the real world works. The first step in addressing this disconnect is to take an honest look at how we think, as individuals and as leaders.

How does thinking work? And how do we move from ingesting information to actually knowing something about the world? We've all experienced a dud teacher who thinks that somehow by reading his lecture notes out loud, he is imparting his knowledge to us. But of course he's not. The same is true of any leader in any organization: If you just state your vision over and over in your town hall addresses or post vision signs on your walls, do your employees truly get it? Nope. That's because of one critical distinction: although we can transfer information, we cannot transfer knowledge to someone else.

Let's break this down.

1. Information is data.
2. Thinking is the process of structuring information to make it useful.
3. Knowledge (also known as a mental model) is built when you structure information to give it meaning.

Looking at this as a simple equation can help make these complex ideas more accessible.

Information + Thinking = Knowledge

Albeit simple, this equation debunks the existing paradigm that taking in information alone is the same as learning. Registering changes in information alone is not learning (a paradigm which explains our obsession with data). What we see is that meaning (mental models) is not an attribute of the data, so changes in data do not equate to changes in meaning! Your ultimate goal as a leader is to enable the individuals on your team to learn, which is going to require them to think. By harnessing the power of their learning, you can continually evolve your organization's mental models to adapt to changing environmental conditions. Expressed as another equation, this concept looks like:

Individual Learning = Changes in Mental Models

Organizational Learning = **Shared** Changes in Mental Models

Let's dig a little deeper into mental models. Although it feels to our conscious self that we interact with the real world directly, in fact we interact indirectly with the real world through our mental models of it. Think of mental models as a lens between you and reality, coloring what you see. Remember (from chapter 1) that we should think of mental models as a lens between us and reality, coloring what we see (Figure 5.1).

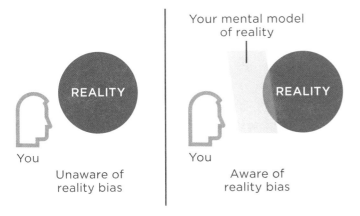

Figure 5.1. Mental models are a lens between you and reality

Whether we construct them as individuals or whether we inherit them as part of our culture, we have the power to shift our mental models. But, first, we need to recognize that we have them.

Dying to Be Barbie

Mental models can be simple or wildly complex. They can describe important or unimportant phenomena. We humans create mental models that summarize and are capable of describing, predicting, and altering behavior. In other words, our mental models may lead us to think certain things about the real world and result in actual behaviors in the real world. Even very dangerous behaviors, like the eating disorders anorexia and bulimia. Let's look at a very familiar example: Barbie.

Mattel's Barbie doll is an icon of female beauty and empowerment in America. Might the mental model of female beauty that Barbie represents have sinister effects? Despite Barbie's professional achievements (stints as a pediatrician, astronaut, and business executive, among them) and her evolution from the blond archetype to more inclusive representations of multicultural beauty, Barbie's design remains problematic. If Barbie were a real woman, her physical proportions would make it impossible for her to lift her head or support her body. At human scale, Barbie's head would be two inches larger and her neck twice as long and six inches thinner than the average American woman's head and neck. Her six-inch ankles and size 3 feet would be unable to support her weight or allow her to balance, forcing her to walk on all fours. Barbie's 16-inch waist would have only enough room for half a liver and a few inches of intestine.[4]

In a study researching the effect of Barbie on young girls' body dissatisfaction, five- to eight-year-old girls were exposed to images of Barbie (US size 2), a more realistic doll (US size 16), or no dolls (baseline control). They were then asked to complete an assessment of body image.

	BARBIE	U.S. average	What are the odds of finding an American woman with Barbie's measurements?
Neck	9"	12-13"	1 in 4,356,203,065
Bust	32"	35-36"	1 in 13
Biceps	7"	10-11"	1 in 6,758
Forearms	6"	9-10"	1 in 18,712
Wrist	3.5"	6-7"	1 in 164,942,740,127
Waist	16"	32-34"	1 in 2,478,756,621
Hips	29"	37-38"	1 in 638,531
Thigh	16"	21-22"	1 in 22,621
Calf	11"	14-15"	1 in 642
Ankle	6"	8-9"	1 in 19,053,353
Waist-Hips ratio			1 in 3,331,259
Bust-Waist ratio			1 in Billions of Billions (impossible odds)
Bust-Hips ratio			1 in 6,280

Figure 5.2: The Barbie mental model is not only improbable, it is in many ways impossible.[5]

The girls who were exposed to Barbie "reported lower body esteem and greater desire for a thinner body shape than girls in the other exposure conditions."[6]

Figure 5.3: Which of these mental models reflects reality?

How might a shift in the mental model of the female form influence children's self-image, behavior, or perception of others? The makers of the Lammily doll decided to create a doll with a key difference: Her proportions were modeled on the average 19-year-old woman. According to the Lammily website, "We believe that if girls are encouraged to follow their dreams, without focusing on what they should look like, then they will grow up to be confident, strong, and powerful women."[7]

Build Teams that Constantly Seek Feedback in Order to Thrive

We want our mental models to reflect the salient aspects of the real-world system or problem we are trying to solve. To determine whether our mental model is accurate, we try it out in the real world and see what happens—that is, we seek *feedback*. If what we expect to occur occurs, this feedback tells us our mental model is well-constructed. If we expect something to occur and it doesn't, this feedback tells us our model needs some work. Either way, we take in these new data, which can inform a continuous process of mental model improvement.

For example, let's say we are leading a new start-up business and we need to zero in on an increasingly refined understanding of who our customer is. As we go out into the world and meet real people, we are learning who is and who isn't our customer based on their interest in our product. Over time, if we notice that all the folks that get excited by our new product are professional and stylish middle-aged men, then we we begin to build a model of our customer: middle-aged male, mid- to high-income, and fashion forward. If, at some point down the road, we are meeting lots of these archetypes who are signaling they don't like the product but lots more who do, then we are getting new feedback from the world: there is a more refined distinction to be made. When middle-aged, mid- to high-income, fashion forward, *rural* men discover our product (say, beard cream), they are unimpressed but when middle-aged, mid- to high-income, fashion forward, *urban* men find it, they buy it. This new signal causes us to update our mental model and the cycle continues.

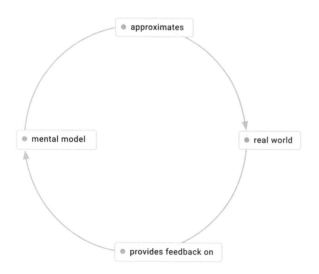

Figure 5.4 Learning is a feedback cycle

This feedback loop between mental models and reality is ever-present in your daily life. When you create a mental model (you are creating them all the time!), you are attempting to describe, summarize, or predict—in summary, to *approximate*—something about the real world. If you're paying attention, the real world will provide feedback in the form of *information* that can: (1) help you to determine the viability of your mental model, (2) select the best mental model among a range of options, or (3) inform how you adapt your mental model. It is this adaptation in response to feedback, at the individual and at the organizational level, that drives success.

Learning, both individual and organizational learning, entails the development of mental models. The models that work (for some purpose that is not always evident to us at the time) survive. Those that don't work, adapt or perish. When we interact with the real world, we receive feedback on the accuracy of our mental models. We must then adjust our mental models based on that feedback, ideally refining our models to be ever-closer approximations of reality. That is learning.

In this way, learning entails unlearning. What is unlearned (possibly in total, usually just partially) is the previously held mental model. Thus, a big part of teaching is making people aware of the lens through which they perceive reality. When you make people aware of their mental models you open them to change. As Claude Bernard said, "It is what we know already that often prevents us from learning."[8]

Figure 5.5: Learning: the feedback loop between reality and our mental models

Learning entails unlearning. What is unlearned (possibly in total, usually just partially) is the previously held mental model. Thus, a big part of teaching is making people aware of the lens through which they perceive reality.

Think of it this way: if we invented human flight but 6 of 10 departing flights crashed before reaching their destination, we would have some work to do. Our mental models of aerodynamics were evidently flawed, based on our low success rate. The crashes are feedback that our mental models are out of alignment with reality because, obviously, we'd hoped to prevent crashes. In this example, individual survival relies on this feedback loop between mental models and the real world. But whole organizations and civilizations rely on it, too. Every organization's survival depends on its ability to learn.

Mental Model	Feedback	Learning
What do we believe to be true?	What does the real world suggest?	How can we update our mental model and adapt to reality?
Example: We develop beard cream for millennial men.	Urban middle-aged men purchase our product.	We develop beard cream for urban Gen Xers.
Your turn:		

Activity 5.1: Learning from feedback

Learning Entails Adaptation

Learning is a process whereby a human being, or group, or organization, or society comes to understand and embody nature's patterns.
—Tom Johnson

As we explained earlier, the need to adapt creates the need for learning. The basic learning process depicted in Figure 5.5

is also the definition of adaptation: the process of changing to become better suited to one's environment. Consider evolution. Like mental models that represent a hypothesis, every organism and species is also a hypothesis—a genetic model—that may or may not turn out to be viable, and therefore experience selective effects and compete with other models. A mutation is, in one sense, a hypothesis that may turn out to be adaptive or maladaptive. If a mutation of longer, pointier beaks appears in birds that eat ants out of deep narrow holes, that hypothesis is adaptive, and the original shorter, fatter beak hypothesis is proven to be maladaptive.

Indeed, our business models work the same way. We come up with hypotheses, concepts, or theories and test them against the real world and see which ones win and which ones lose. Learning, science, adaptation, and evolution are all structurally similar. Each of these phenomena fundamentally involves a model that gets tested against the real world. Selection affects the viability of any model against competing models. There are winners and losers. Learning, both individual and organizational, entails the development of mental models; only the ones that work survive.

Failure Is Feedback

Humans are adept learners: we even learn when things go bad. If at first you don't succeed, fail fast and incorporate the feedback! This is the lesson of Procter & Gamble's introduction of the (now) popular Febreze product.

Created in 1993 by P&G, an odorless, colorless, cheap liquid was marketed to people in a way that promised to remove odor. The more they pitched Febreze as an odor-eliminator, the worse their sales became. Confused by this phenomenon, P&G investigated by speaking to consumers directly. In one instance, researchers spoke with a woman from Phoenix, Arizona, who proudly exclaimed that her house smelled fine even though she had nine cats (while to the newcomers her house smelled strongly of cats). Combining psychology with fast failing, the researchers discovered the phenomenon they now reference in their advertisements: going "noseblind."[9] They coined the term to describe when people develop habits that desensitize them to certain smells—much like muscle memory, but specific to nose.

It then became clear that Febreze wasn't selling as an odor-eliminator because consumers didn't think that their homes had a bad smell. Having rooted out the problem, P&G accepted their failure and began to work toward a new solution. After recording interviews of their customers, their researchers realized that people seemed proud of their work once they finished cleaning. But it took one specific comment for P&G to finally discover their new angle. After making her bed, one woman stood back, appreciated her work, and then sprayed it with Febreze. In the interview she said, "It's nice, you know? Spraying feels like a little mini-celebration when I'm done with a room."[10]

Researchers realized that if they marketed Febreze as a reward for cleaning or as the finishing touch to a clean room, they could tap into the consumer habits and sentiments. Instead of trying to get people to develop new habits by cleaning with Febreze, they used the psychology of cue and reward in order to augment existing habits. The cue was identified as a freshly cleaned room, closely followed by the routine spraying with Febreze, and the reward was "a smell that says you've done a great job."[11]

No one likes being told they have a smelly home, but everyone loves a cherry-on-top closure. After initially losing millions of dollars, Febreze was newly marketed in the summer of 1998, and within two months sales doubled. By the following year, Febreze revenues reached $230 million.[12]

Without P&G's ability to fail fast and learn from mistakes, Febreze would have been terminated and its potential forgotten. Instead of accepting defeat—or worse, ignoring it—P&G asked a simple yet difficult question: "Why did we fail?" Not only must companies be willing to fail, they must then ask hard questions of themselves and their customers, and scrupulously apply the feedback. In this way, organizational failures can be as powerful as successes. This painstaking process of investigation and reflection allowed for new discoveries and a re-direction that saved Febreze. More important, we can still see these valuable lessons being applied at P&G with the booming revival of their product Old Spice in 2010.[13]

The Power of Sharing Mental Models: Wow Stories

"I am empowered to create unique, memorable and personal experiences for our guests." This simple employee statement (number 3 on the Ritz-Carlton's list of 12 service values)[14] exemplifies a culture in which employees are empowered to learn. Ritz-Carlton, one of the world's most recognized luxury hotel chains, with 90 hotels and resorts around the world, uses organizational learning to drive its award-winning customer service. They do so by building capacity through institutionalized processes they call Daily Line-Ups and Wow Stories that use the power of storytelling as a way to spread learning across the organization.

At 9 every morning, Ritz-Carlton employees (referred to as "ladies and gentlemen") meet for their 15-minute Daily Line-Up.[15] All employees, irrespective of position, meet to discuss their wins and losses, and to share their own stories. Empowered by the Gold Standards of the company, employees are encouraged to share stories in which they created a wow moment for a guest. Wow Stories range from small personal moments to complex and involved displays of caring. As long as the intention is genuine and the action instills pride, employees are empowered by the company to create these memorable moments. And that's exactly what they are: memorable. For example:

A couple traveled to Seoul, Korea to adopt the newest member of their family... After the couple completed the adoption, they brought their new son with them to the hotel. The Guest Relations Agent heard the mother speaking to her son one morning and realized that they were having trouble communicating because the mother knew very little Korean. The Guest Relations Agent helped the mother by translating several common English baby words into Korean. This enabled the mother to quickly and easily communicate with her son when he was hungry or tired...They expressed their thanks, saying that they would leave the hotel with many happy memories of their new family.[16]

While the ultimate goal is to provide amazing customer service (successful mission moments), the organizational learning goal is to promote a culture of learning. Between 70% and 90% of organizational learning is informal.[17] *Informal learning* is loosely defined as consisting mostly of experiential learning and the sharing of these moments. Studies show that humans are easily influenced by stories and perceptions. At the same time, we celebrate stories in which the underdog creates moments of genuine success and we disassociate with stories of higher-ups misbehaving.[18]

Acts of thoughtful customer service create memorable moments for guests. They are also a powerful source of learning for the ladies and gentlemen of the Ritz-Carlton. This is in part because Wow Stories are not merely shared in Daily Line-Ups, the best Wow Stories "rise to the top" and are then made available through their intranet (internal website) and video productions; some even become organization-wide policies or practices. This bottom-up learning influences the entire organization—that's organizational learning in practice. The Ritz-Carlton has seen the positive effects of their Wow Stories for years, and recent research reveals the significance of not creating positive customer service moments: a whopping 67% of customers leave because of the bad attitude of one employee.[19] As the customer service industry struggles with their satisfaction ratings, the Ritz-Carlton's ratings remain steadily high.

Not only does the Ritz-Carlton engage their employees through the Wow Stories, they create learning opportunities. Leaders can't stop with simply sharing these success stories, they have to create the culture and environment that allows them to take root and manifest naturally. Joe Quitoni, corporate director of culture transformation at The Ritz-Carlton Leadership Center, highlights "genuine," "personal," and "always" as key aspects of the Gold Standards; respect and authenticity must flow both ways. As a result, the Ritz-Carlton enjoys one of the industry's lowest employee turnover rates.[20]

Learning Organizations

We've talked a bit about how we learn from feedback. But what distinguishes a learning organization? In simplest terms, learning is the continuous modification of mental models based on feedback from the external environment. A learning organization is an organization in which the natural function of learning is directed toward vision, mission, and capacity. In our experience working with leaders of organizations large and small, learning is the function that poses the greatest challenge for them. Nothing—neither inside nor outside the organization—is static. You might have the best organizational plan in the world and implement it well, but without the ability to adapt all organisms, humans, and organizations would fail. Organizations, like any living organism, must learn in order to adapt to the changing environment, to survive, and to thrive.[21]

Learning entails unlearning. What is unlearned is the previously held mental model. Thus, a big part of teaching is making people aware of the lens through which they perceive reality.

Though there is a wealth of earlier work on organizational learning, the concept of the "learning organization" was indisputably catapulted into public consciousness by Peter Senge's 1990 book, *The Fifth Discipline*. Senge wrote that learning organizations are "...organizations where people continually expand their capacity to create the results they truly desire, where new and expansive patterns of thinking are nurtured, where collective aspiration is set free, and where people are continually learning to see the whole together."[22]

This construct obviously has tremendous appeal, as scholars and practitioners alike have paid homage to the idea of the learning organization for a quarter century.

At the same time, few experts speak in concrete terms about learning organization characteristics, let alone offer clear and practical ideas to create such an organization. As management philosopher Margaret Wheatley explained:

> Many organizations are now trying to walk under the banner of The Learning Organization, realizing that knowledge is our most important product...But the only place that I've seen it is in the Army. As one colonel said, 'We realized a while ago that it's better to learn than be dead.'[23]

This lack of shared understanding of the term has fostered different views of what a learning organization is, resulting in such extreme definitions as:[24]

[being] like a living organism, consisting of empowered, motivated employees, living in a clearly perceived symbiosis, sharing the feeling of a common destiny and profit, striving towards jointly defined goals, anxious to use every opportunity to learn from situations, processes and competition in order to adapt harmoniously to the changes in their environment and to improve continuously their own and their company's competitive performance;[25]

and

an aspiration often viewed cynically by staff who don't believe the rhetoric is sincere.[26]

David A. Garvin wrote about Senge's prescriptions for creating a learning organization in a 1993 piece in the *Harvard Business Review*.

Sound idyllic? Absolutely. Desirable? Without question. But does it provide a framework for action? Hardly. The recommendations are far too abstract, and too many questions remain unanswered. How, for example, will managers know when their companies have become learning organizations. What concrete changes in behavior are required? What policies and programs must be in place. How do you get from here to there? Most discussions of learning organizations finesse these issues. Their focus is high philosophy and grand themes, sweeping metaphors rather than gritty details of practice.

Garvin advocates an "actionable and easy to apply" definition of learning organizations, "clearer guidelines for practice, filled with operational advice," and "better tools for assessing an organization's rate and level of learning."[27]

To this we say, game on! We have enabled countless learning organizations by drawing on the most rigorous research in the field and building our own technological tools to solve these very problems.

Learn by Example

One of the specific and practical things you can do to build a culture of mental models is to get the entire leadership team to assume another as leaders of learning. The CEO must also serve as a Chief Learning Officer (CLO). This dual role is required not just of CEOs but of any leader across the organization. If managers make learning a priority, others will see it as a priority, too. Effective leaders are skilled "lead learners" adroit at inculcating culture (facilitating shared understanding of key mental models).

The best chef (the executive chef or CEO) in a Michelin-starred restaurant often doesn't do any of the cooking. Seems like a paradox, right? If she's not cooking, what is she doing?

She's standing at "the pass," expediting, prioritizing, and communicating orders as they come in; exercising quality control by ensuring that the fish isn't overcooked, the side dish is ample, and the final plating of the dish is aesthetically pleasing. She monitors plates as they are being bussed and returned—are they clean or barely touched? Are they returned with a complaint? Finally, the executive chef's most important job is to ensure the sous, meat, sides, and pastry chefs learn. She knows that the safety of her Michelin stars rests not on her own ability to cook, but on her team's ability to meet her exacting standards. When leaders focus on learning, they communicate that it's an organizational priority and build and incentivize a culture of learning.

Figure out what the pass looks like in your organization (we've seen some cool ones!) and lead from it. It need not be a physical pass, like in a restaurant, but it does require analogous functionality.

Organizational learning involves everyone in the organization, but the spark for it must come from leaders (formal and informal) at all levels of the organization.

Otherwise, employees will see it as an unnecessary and temporary initiative that they can "ride out."

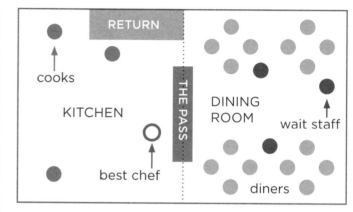

MICHELIN STAR KITCHEN

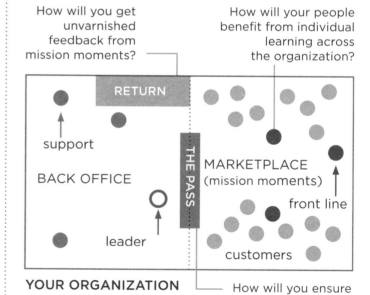

YOUR ORGANIZATION

Figure 5.6: Leaders of organizational learning lead from the pass

Structure/Function	The Pass How will you ensure mission moments go well?	The Return How will you get unvarnished feedback from mission moments?	Teach and Learn How will your people benefit from individual learning across the organization?
Michelin-Starred Kitchen	Expediting and plating (quality control of meal)	Seeing what comes back on the dishes (how clean are the plates?) is unvarnished feedback as to how diners enjoyed meal	Continuously learn what works and what doesn't and act as teacher for other chefs to develop them into Michelin Star-worthy chefs
Your Organization			

Activity 5.2: What does the pass look like in your organization?

Check #18: We Train People to Think in Order to Learn

Organizational leaders often get promoted up the ranks for what they can do; because they are competent. But at a certain point it's not about what you can do anymore, it's about what you can teach and inspire others to do. Great leaders and managers make the transition from skilled doer to skilled teacher because they (like Jack Welch) know that learning is the real source of an organization's competitive advantage. The goal of any CEO should be to create "distal CEOs"— people at the end of the tentacle arms of an organization dealing with customers, suppliers, and partners who have shared mental models that guide them through the all-important mission moments. People whose thoughts and actions indicate ownership in the organization. Leaders need to create individuals who are constantly learning and adapting according to information on the ground. As Mike Curtis, Airbnb Vice President of Engineering explains, "We believe in shaping good judgment in individuals instead of imposing rules across the team."[28]

Standard job training is insufficient: learning how to perform a task in accordance with policies and procedures will not generate the type of adaptive, think-on-their feet employees your company needs in order to interface with a changing external environment. Not only do they need to provide a stellar

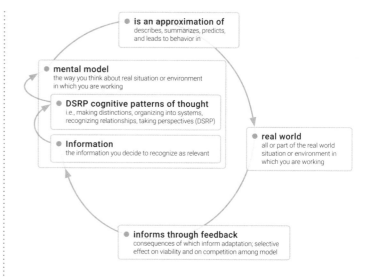

Figure 5.7: Mental models consolidate the meaning we make when we organize information using DSRP (mental model = information + thinking)

customer experience, they are a critical source of information for the organization. They must excel at thinking in order to excel at learning. Organizational leaders, policymakers, and leaders in business and education continuously call for the creation of lifelong learners and learning organizations. Why are we not calling for more *thinking*? Thinking is the driver for all learning.

It's important to remember that all organisms, including humans (alone or in groups), learn—they interact in various ways with the environment, observe the real-world feedback that results, and then adapt their understanding of things to somehow incorporate or accommodate the new information. As both a leader and a learner, you don't have to do anything to cause learning: it is a naturally occurring process. So you can relax. As Sugata Mitra explains, "We need to look at learning as the product of educational self-organization. It's not about making learning happen; it's about letting it happen."[29] In fact, it is likely that your employees will learn many things you wish they wouldn't. For example, if your behavior contradicts publicly espoused values, employees will learn to take your words with a grain of salt and pay more attention to your behavior. If you sanction employees for making mistakes and fail to promote a culture that rewards risk-taking, your employees (and your organization) will learn from that, too. They will learn to be risk-averse and they'll avoid innovation and creativity in favor of safe bets. So let learning happen, but not just any learning. *You must direct learning toward increasing capacity to do your mission to achieve your vision.*

Figure 5.8: Alignment between learning and capacity completes the strong VMCL chain

Thinking Drives Learning and Learning Drives the Organization

The growth and increased reliance on technology and automation is dramatically changing the nature of work and makes organizational learning absolutely critical. New jobs increasingly require rapid and creative thinking and high levels of social and emotional intelligence.[30] These requirements won't be met by existing training programs; instead, they illustrate the need to teach thinking (and metacognition) and *how to learn.*

Learning isn't something you do only in school, it is lifelong and constant. It is something you do to solve real problems in the real world. Learning is fundamentally what it means to be human. All organisms learn in order to survive and thrive. Similarly, all organizations learn. That means that learning isn't just a good thing to do, but a fundamentally essential function of all organizations. Learning is what makes everything else work. Learning is what makes your people and your organization as a whole capable of adapting.

But creating a learning organization isn't the same as creating a training and development system in which people have opportunities to better themselves (such as can taking online or live courses). You might need one of those, too, but don't confuse that with organizational learning. Organizational learning means that you transform your workforce into a dynamic thinkforce, a swarm of thinking individuals who solve problems by building better mental models, sharing and evolving them, and ultimately building capacity to do your mission better to achieve your vision.

Learning Is the Engine of Your Organization

We are not fans of using triangles to illustrate organizations. Mostly because they often are used in ways that indicate that things are simpler than they really are. But we'll make an exception and use a triangle here because it does a good job of visually explaining the most important takeaway from this chapter: thinking is the foundation that drives it all. Getting the right talent and then giving them the freedom, resources, training, tools, and technology to do their best thinking is job #1.

Of course, job #2 is to build a culture that recognizes mental models; has a way to think about them (distinctions, systems, relationships, and perspectives); and can express them, build, share and evolve them. This will bring about both individual and organizational learning, which is the crux of creating an adaptive organization and also drives increased capacity to do the mission and bring about the vision.

Leaders must direct individual learning, with a focus on metacognition (understanding one's thinking—associated with EQ and IQ) and systems thinking (since organizations both consist of and operate within systems). As part of this, leaders must differentiate between receiving information, and building knowledge by structuring that information. Organizational learning begins with the learning done by individuals, but leadership is required to ensure learning does not end there.

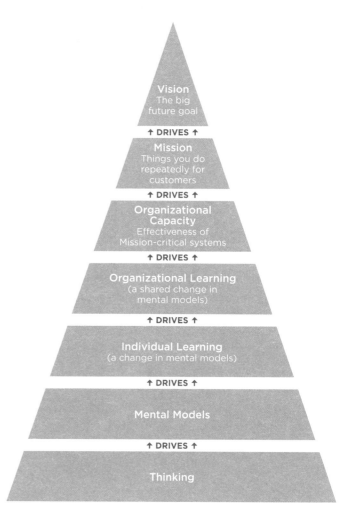

Figure 5.9: Another way of saying thinking makes vision possible

Thinking About Thinking: Systems Thinking

So how do you structure information to facilitate the identification and creation of mental models? How do you help your team think in order to learn? Throughout many years of research, we have identified four simple, logical rules for structuring information: make **distinctions** and identify **systems**, **relationships**, and **perspectives**. As you already know, we call this DSRP.[31] In order to explain them, we'll look at them individually. But like the four base pairs of DNA—which, with alterations in their sequence can make up organisms ranging from a person to a platypus—these rules can be combined and recombined in infinite ways to form myriad complex structures. Figure 5.10 illustrates the four underlying patterns of metacognition (distinctions, systems, relationships, and perspectives [DSRP]) that drive all of these types of cognitive and affective learning and thinking.

DISTINCTIONS   SYSTEMS   RELATIONSHIPS   PERSPECTIVES

Figure 5.10: Systems thinking/DSRP are metacognitive patterns that lie at the root of the many other types of thinking we all want employees to possess.

DISTINCTIONS

It is innate for humans to distinguish one thing from another. But we often do this unconsciously and without considering the implications of the distinctions we are drawing. Distinctions consist of two elements: the *identity* (the thing or idea that is the focus of attention) and the *other* (that which is *not* the identity). To deliberately make distinctions, we ask:

What is_____?

What is not _____?

How might you distinguish between _____and _____?

How might you compare and contrast _____ with _____?

Conscious, systematic application of the distinctions rule increases the clarity and precision of your thinking, eliminates redundancy, and promotes awareness of perspective (since what we focus on is always a matter of perspective—we'll get to that shortly). On the other hand, unconscious distinction-making can lead to marginalizing the other and a lack of awareness of the sources and the consequences of our boundary-making.

SYSTEMS

Any idea or thing can be split into parts or lumped into a whole. In identifying systems, we ask:

What are the parts of_____?

What is_____a part of?

What are the parts of the relationship between_____ and_____?

What are the parts of_____when looked at from the viewpoint of_____?

When we apply the systems rule, we recognize that what is a *part* of one whole can also be a *whole* in itself composed of different parts. The way we organize parts into wholes is influenced by perspective and can change the characteristics of the system.

So far, so good. The next two rules are a little more subtle, and can take a bit longer to flesh out.

RELATIONSHIPS

The relationships rule—any idea or thing can be related to any other idea or thing—is characterized by two elements: *action* and *reaction*. When problem solving, we often look for relationships of correlation, some of which may involve cause and effect. Systems thinking often emphasizes the complexity of relationships, seeking out webs of causality rather than single, linear causes. To think through relationships, we ask:

What ideas are related to _____ and what ideas are related by_____?
What idea relates _____ and _____?
How are the parts of _____ related?
How are the parts of _____ related to the parts of _____?
What are the relationships among _____ and _____ and other things?

Thorough application of the relationships rule requires identifying the relationship. For example, global warming could be identified as the cause of rising sea levels. Alternatively, the relationship between two people might be identified as romantic, platonic, boss-subordinate, or perhaps even "Mary" (if Mary introduced them). Much of the complexity and many of the unique properties we see at the group level are attributable to the relationships among the constituent parts of a whole. Since they are often the hidden dynamics of systems, identifying the relationships among parts of the whole is critical to systems thinking.

PERSPECTIVES

This rule entails two elements: a *point* (that which is doing the seeing or focusing) and a *view* (that which is being focused upon or seen). Any thing or idea can be either the point or the view of a perspective. To pin down perspectives, we ask:

What are the parts of the viewpoint _____ when looking at _____?
How are _____ and _____ related when looking at them from a new perspective?
Can you think of _____ from multiple perspectives?
What are the parts of _____ when looked at from multiple viewpoints?

Conscious application of the perspectives rule requires that we acknowledge that what we *perceive* as reality is really a mental model—just one of many ways to frame information—and proceed to identify the perspective(s) that make up that model (more on that in a minute). Perspective-taking is involved in every distinction we make and every system and relationship we identify. The ability to identify the perspectives implicit in all information we encounter—and to consider and apply alternative perspectives—is a tremendous aid in problem-solving and consensus-building. In other words, we need to look at how we (and others) frame issues, consciously or unknowingly. *When we change the way we look at things, the things we look at change.*

While these thinking questions can be used to think through any content or problem, they are built into the underlying structure of Plectica maps (see page 144-145) so that you don't need to remember anything to use them. Let's apply these four simple ideas to maps. For example, we can make distinctions by labeling "cards" in the map, such as in the map below where we distinguish "Sales and Marketing function" or, alternatively, distinguish these as two separate functions. It is your choice how you do it, but the thinking behind these two mental models is different.

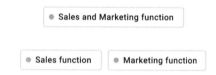

Figure 5.11: Which distinction do you want to make?

We could use systems (part/whole) to create a slightly different model that combines the two mental models in Figure 5.11. Note that the Sales and Marketing functions are still distinct objects, but are now *part* of the larger combined Sales and Marketing function as shown in Figure 5.12.

Figure 5.12: Parts of a larger whole

Let's look at a more complex part/whole system like the qualities needed to fill a new Product Manager position. Figure 5.13 shows that there are three main types of skills we seek: intuitive, deep, and methodological skills, each of which are broken down into further parts. We use this full understanding of what we are seeking in our hiring process, and ultimately, have a higher likelihood of finding the right candidate.

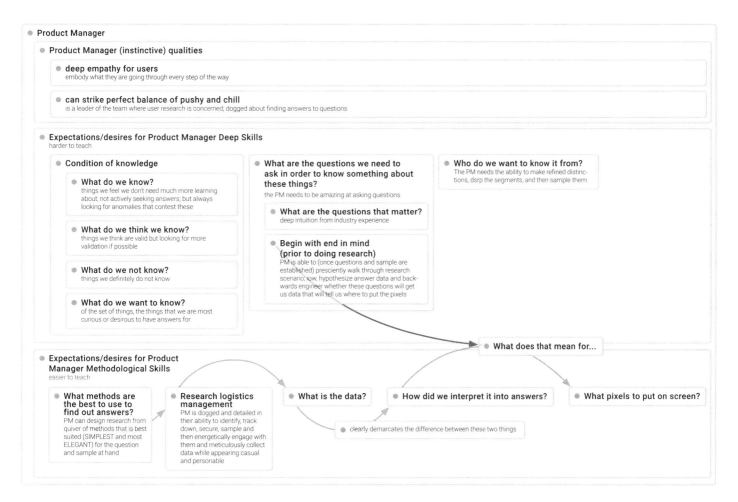

Figure 5.13: Thinking through the parts of the Product Manager position we want to hire.

We often need to consider the relationship between and among things to better understand them. Figure 5.14 questions the relationship between the Engineering team and the Customer, by simply adding a relational line between the two:

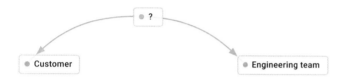

Figure 5.14: A relationship exists between the Engineering team and the Customer (but what is it)?

Note that our mental model shows that there is a relationship between the Engineering team and the Customer but it doesn't stipulate what that relationship is. If we distinguish the relationship (R) by making it a distinction (D) we call "product manager," we also now see that this relationship is *actually the function* of the Product Manager!

Figure 5.15: The Product Manager is the relationship between the Engineering team and the Customer.

And if we mix and match the components of DSRP a bit more we can add parts to better understand our distinction (D), the product manager, whose function is to be the relationship (R) between two departments: For example, the parts of the job of project manager (from our earlier map) can be added to this relationship.

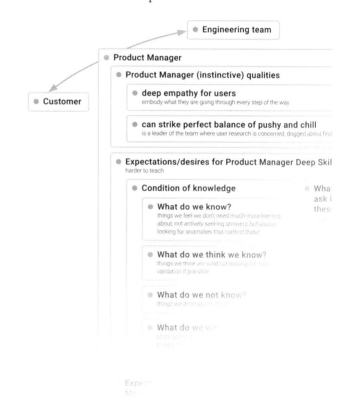

Figure 5.16: The Product Manager is a system and also a relationship between the Engineering team and the Customer.

We might then use perspectives (P) to think about the software from the points-of-view of the Product Manager, the Customer, the Engineering team, and Sales and Marketing.

also provides a universal language for communicating mental models. This facilitates organizational learning: brainstorming, innovation, and forecasting for even the largest and

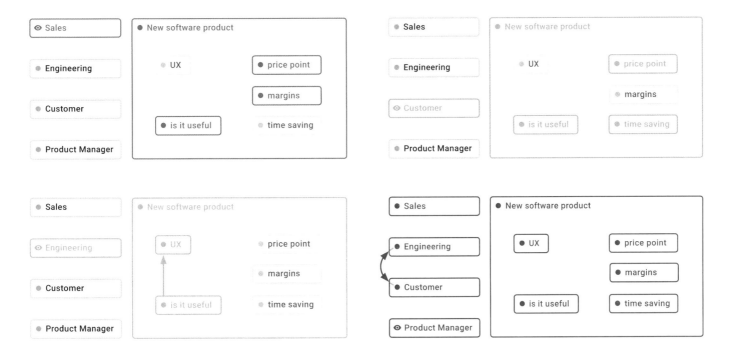

Figure 5.17: A map showing the different mental models (perspectives) that different groups have about the same software

Applying each rule to any problem allows us to identify and explore unmade distinctions, systems, and relationships, and to take perspectives not yet taken. Thinking through DSRP

occupationally differentiated organization because it creates a shared language about our thinking and the mental models we build. Otherwise, employees from different occupations may share more culture with their fellow engineers, let's say, than with nonengineer co-workers.[32] This shared process also generates metrics on learning and collaboration that allow leaders to compare learning across groups with different functions and foci.

Check #19: We Constantly Evolve Our Mental Models

It is the purposeful sharing and evolving of mental models that makes learning an ongoing process within an organization. Learning must be an organizational goal, so leadership must create systems to encourage, capture, and disseminate both individual and collaborative learning. This entails generating evergreen institutional knowledge, which much be constantly shared, evolved, and distributed.

The largest worldwide study of employee engagement was conducted by Gallup. The study isolated the top 12 key management practices for sustaining workplace excellence. One of these top determinants—positive employee responses to the statement "This last year, I have had opportunities at work to learn and grow"—was linked to almost every business outcome Gallup studied. Employees with the most learning opportunities were twice as likely to spend their career with their companies.[33] In a report offering multidisciplinary explanations for the well-documented human need to learn, thrive, and progress, business management authors Rodd Wagner and Jim Harter summarize their findings on what they call the "twelfth element:"

> When employees feel like they are learning and growing, they work harder and more efficiently. [Employee

learning/growth]...has a particularly strong connection to customer engagement and profitability...These superior customer relationships and profits may occur because [the study finds these] employees who are learning and genuinely interested in their work have better ideas.[34]

Encouragement, access, and adaptation of institutional knowledge is key when it comes to creating the systems to generate organizational learning capacity. In fact, much of your work as a leader will be to implement, constantly assess, and improve a learning system. One Gallup business report on the value of organizational learning describes "learning bottlenecks:"

> A company can be chock-full of brilliant learners, but their talent is wasted if the company's leadership doesn't want to, or doesn't have a system in place, to hear it. A similar result comes from a lack of shared vision. Useful information and innovative ideas may be obtained, but they are useless if no one uses or implements the intelligence.[35]

Thus, a critical element of any learning system is the distribution of both the responsibility for and the fruits of learning.

There are numerous reasons to focus on organizational learning, all backed by research. Most important, Bersin by Deloitte Consulting has conducted extensive research demonstrating that the all-important factor of employee engagement is most affected by whether an employee is continuously learning and developing in his or her career.[36]

OutThink, OutSync, OutDo, OutLast

Now that you have given your team the tools of systems thinking, how do you engage your employees in your business around these ideas? Systems mapping enables you to harness and capture the creativity, perspective, and collaboration of your entire team. The basic steps in the systems mapping process are quite simple, and are therefore easy to use as an individual or as a team. Although there are many mapping softwares available, all of which can be used to map and understand systems, we use Plectica software in our examples for the ease of continuity with the theoretical underpinnings articulated in this book.

Plectica mapping software was born out of our research lab to facilitate and motivate systems thinking through the use of a practical, visual tool that would allow anyone to get the benefits of systems thinking/DSRP without investing a lot of time in learning it. The name Plectica is derived from the term *plectics* which is the name Nobel laureate Murray Gell-Mann gave to the field of study that attempts to understand complex adaptive systems (like your organization, or your thought processes, or a flocks of birds). Gell-Mann thought the name was important because it connected with:

...both simplicity and complexity. What is most exciting about our work is that it illuminates the chain of connections between, on the one hand, the simple underlying laws that govern the behavior of all matter in the universe and, on the other hand, the complex fabric that we see around us, exhibiting diversity, individuality, and evolution. The interplay between simplicity and complexity is the heart of our subject.

It is interesting to note, therefore, that the two words are related. The Indo-European root *plek- gives rise to the Latin verb *plicare*, <u>to fold</u>, which yields *simplex*, literally <u>once folded</u>, from which our English word "simple" derives. But *plek- likewise gives the Latin past participle *plexus*, <u>braided</u> or <u>entwined</u>, from which is derived *complexus*, literally <u>braided together</u>, responsible for the English word "complex." The Greek equivalent to *plexus* is πλεκτος (*plektos*), yielding the mathematical term "symplectic," which also has the literal meaning <u>braided together</u>, but comes to English from Greek rather than Latin.

The name that I propose for our subject is "plectics," derived, like mathematics, ethics, politics, economics, and so on, from the Greek. Since *plektos* with no prefix comes from *plek-, but without any commitment to the notion of "once" as in "simple" or to the notion of "together" as in "complex," the derived word "plectics" can cover both simplicity and complexity.[37]

Plectica software is extremely simple yet complexity-friendly. Built on the science of complexity, where complex adaptive systems have simple rules underneath, Plectica maps are built on individual "cards" that can form a larger more complex network of cards. Each card has rules.

- Distinctions Rule: Each card can be distinct from other cards
- Systems Rule: Each card can have sub-parts or be part of other cards
- Relationships Rule: Any card can be related to any other card
- Perspectives Rule: Any card can be a perspective on other cards

The most important rule is the fifth rule—the Mix-and-Match Rule states: Any card can combine the four rules in any way. We think of this as the rule that tells us that: *anything can do anything to anything.*

Somewhat amazingly, using these four simple rules, Plectica maps can model ANY idea, no matter how simple or complex and no matter the subject. We make it our mission to help people to build powerful maps of their ideas (mental models). Importantly, the simple rules that underlie these maps also make it possible for Plectica to provide structural suggestions to improve your ideas. We see this as providing organizations with four critical values and benefits.

1. **OutThink:** Use maps backed by cognitive science to organize and explain just about anything. Map your ideas to more deeply understand your work, systems, processes, or challenges—and make better decisions for your organization more often. OutThink your competition by breaking down existing mental models, shaping new ones, and adapting to new, changing contexts. And, improve your ideas with structural thinking using DSRP. Overall, think with greater clarity and build better ideas by outthinking the competition.

2. **OutSync:** Get everyone on the same page (literally) by presenting your ideas with clarity and fidelity, and fostering communication and teamwork. This includes real-time collaboration and communication with colleagues, where everyone's ideas are captured in one place. Create a shared mental model to ensure you build, learn and grow together as a team. Use synchronous and asynchronous collaborative mapping to build knowledge (learn) together. Work better together sharing and evolving mental models and you will outsync the competition.

3. **OutDo:** Design, execute, and integrate workflows to bring ideas into action. Use your maps to create and assign tasks and keep actions (how/what) closely aligned with purpose (why). Work smarter and more effectively, not harder and you'll outdo the competition.

4. **OutLast:** Adapt to the VUCA environment. Develop more adaptive thinkers and transform your workforce into a thinkforce. Transform your organization into an adaptive learning organization. OutThinking, OutSyncing, and OutDoing will ensure you survive and thrive and beat the competition through increased adaptivity.

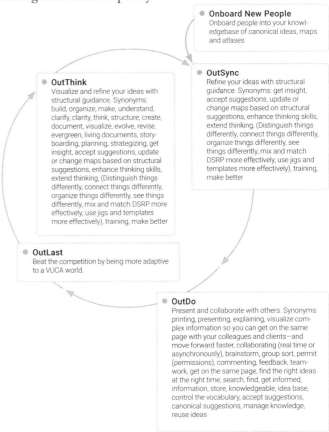

Figure 5.18: OutThink, OutSync, OutDo, OutLast

OutThink: Map Ideas to Improve Ideas

Plectica is designed to help you build better ideas by mapping your problems, workflows, systems, processes, or challenges. Plectica's powerful architecture can be extended to an infinite degree of complexity, yet you can get started immediately and without too much effort. The architecture and features encourage you to do several important things that will lead to better thinking, better maps, and higher impact.

Plectica helps us structure our thoughts to get to these improvements. DSRP is embedded into the functionality of the software. These four simple, logical rules for structuring information apply to any topic or issue, and offer a robust method to interrogate your ideas from conception through every iteration of development. The cognitive science that backs systems thinking allows you to organize and explain just about anything.

Let's take this example: you notice something in your daily work that isn't working. Start by mapping how the process currently works, what the steps are, the workflow, and some of the assumptions that went into this workflow at its inception. As you map, apply the cognitive rules for structuring information:

Distinctions Rule: *What are the main ideas?* Create separate cards to distinguish the main ideas (each possible component of the process) and clarify the workflow process. Get the right top-level ideas on your map; all that you need and none that you don't.

Systems Rule: *What are the parts?* Break down the main ideas into parts. Organize and group the cards to analyze the multiple parts of the system.

Relationships Rule: *What are the relationships?* Label the relationships between and among the main ideas, between and among the parts. Draw arrows between cards to identify webs of causality that connect them.

Perspectives Rule: *How would your map change if you took a different perspective?* Consider and apply alternative points of view by exploring what different cards (people or things) see and don't see. When you change the way you look at things, the things you look at change.

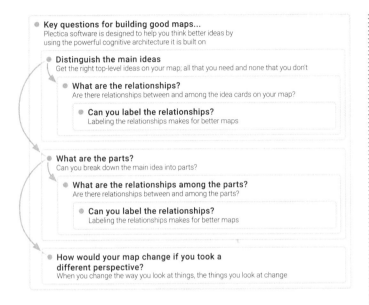

Key questions for building good maps...
Plectica software is designed to help you think better ideas by
using the powerful cognitive architecture it is built on

Distinguish the main ideas
Get the right top-level ideas on your map; all that you need and none that you don't

What are the relationships?
Are there relationships between and among the idea cards on your map?

Can you label the relationships?
Labeling the relationships makes for better maps

What are the parts?
Can you break down the main idea into parts?

What are the relationships among the parts?
Are there relationships between and among the parts?

Can you label the relationships?
Labeling the relationships makes for better maps

**How would your map change if you took a
different perspective?**
When you change the way you look at things, the things you look at change

Figure 5.19: Plectica's cognitive architecture
enhances thinking and clarity

Think of this initial map as your first draft. Improving ideas often involves re-visiting our original work and refining the thinking, until we have the best expression of our work. No one is perfect. And neither is any map: regroup cards, define previously implicit relationships, add new cards. An iterative systems mapping process will allow you to break down the existing mental model of your workflow processes, and shape a new one that is based in reality. Deep understanding and clarity about your work, systems, processes, or challenges evolves over time and through collaboration. You OutThink your competition as you move deeper into the complexity of your ideas and make transformative changes to the systems you model (see OutDo: Aligning Maps to Action).

The seed of an idea can come from anything at anytime, anywhere in your organization. It should spark the process of building a map of the system of interest. Depending on the complexity of the idea, mapping might involve building a single small map, or a very large and involved map, or many maps linked together in what we call an atlas—a collection of overlapping, adjacent, or reference maps that are key for understanding a particular process or problem, department or organization. Maps that you create are added to your personal library in the software and can be linked together to form larger concepts and atlases. All of these items can remain private in your personal libraries or made public for collaborative libraries.

The process of mapping is based on the cognitive science of how we think. Prior to deeper studies in neuroscience and cognition, scientists didn't understand how they were built or aligned with real-world systems. Through our research, we have come to understand the cognitive code that structures our mental models (making distinctions, organizing part-whole systems, recognizing relationships, and taking perspectives). Based on this research, we know that we can transform how we frame, design, predict and react to real-world events that are universal to all systemic thinking. Knowing this science, we can use it to our advantage to think differently, and OutThink the competition.

The Science of Cognition and Visual Mapping

Italian physician and educator, Maria Montessori, explained that thinking is "expressed by the hands before it can be put into words."[38] Visual mapping allows you to express your thinking. Research shows that visual mapping enhances meaningful learning, such that in the end mappers better understand their thinking on a topic or issue (see Figure 5.20[39]).[40]

The work of Eden and colleagues suggested that "it is often the process of reflective mapping that gives mapping it's utility".[41,42] Constructing a map requires one to make one's understanding of a concept explicit.

An explicit model of visual mapping—concept mapping—was born out of Joseph Novak's program out of Cornell University in 1972 to better an individual's conceptual understanding of topics, and observe explicit changes in the concepts and the structures that underlie those concepts. Novak's lab found through research with both children and adults that "meaningful learning was the most important factor in building powerful knowledge and structures" as opposed to learning by rote. Concept maps, based on cognitive theory, help individuals learn meaningfully.[43] Also at Cornell, the Cabrera's took the field of visual cognitive mapping significantly further with DSRP-maps, by providing the underlying rules of knowledge formation and metacognition.

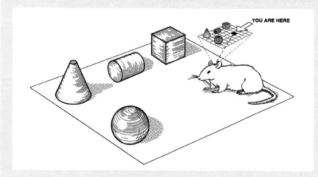

Figure 5.20: Cognitive mapping of real-domains

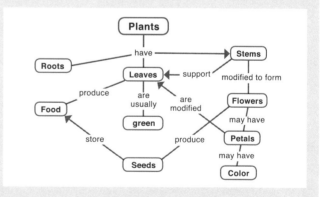

Figure 5.21: A concept map in the style of Joseph Novak

OutSync: Share Ideas

Plectica increases the speed with which ideas evolve and get better by providing a collaborative space to help individuals and teams evolve the maps as new thinking or new information becomes available. Sharing maps and collaborating with colleagues in real time is critically important to remaining viable in a dynamic, VUCA environment. Visual systems maps not only facilitate communication, teamwork, and discussion, but also ensure that everyone shares the same mental model of an idea, system of ideas, process, or phenomenon.

Visual systems maps not only facilitate communication, teamwork, and discussion, but also ensure that everyone shares the same mental model of an idea, system of ideas, process, or phenomenon.

Shared mental models across your team or organization is even easier with the convenience of having everyone's ideas captured in one place. The map is a common touch point for discussing ideas, issues, or challenges and improving them in real time, with each following the same simple rules of DSRP. Systems maps are ideal for collaborating both in person and online. All maps are shared using a simple link and can be accessed by as many collaborators as you like, even all at the same time. On any given map, everyone involved can see everyone else's cursor to simplify communication about the ideas—much like sharing ideas on a whiteboard, but in a more dynamic, flexible way (see Figure 5.22). The syncing functionality of the software is key to getting on the same page and staying there.

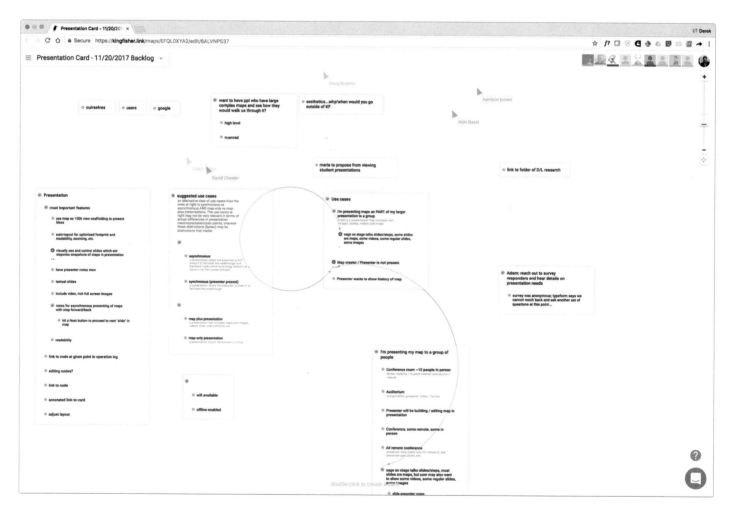

Figure 5.22: A meeting swarm occurs when a synchronous collaboration map facilitates discussion (in person or virtual) in real time

Blue highlighted text shows Doug's contributions

Pink highlighted text shows Daniel's contributions

Figure 5.23: Ideas and learning are collaborative and can be either synchronous or asynchronous

Figure 5.23 shows that collaboration allows tracking of who added what and can occur either in real time or asynchronously. It is helpful to be able to see who contributed what in order to better understand their perspective

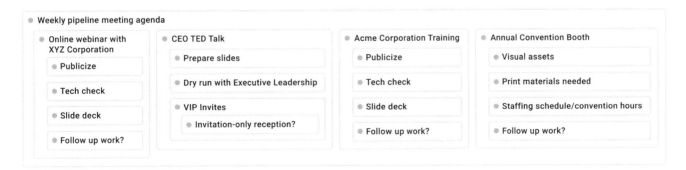

Figure 5.24: Map of a weekly meeting agenda

We've found that visual systems maps are also great tools to use for managing the agenda of work across scale, from a single meeting to a team project to the company's mission. Maps are great for creating or co-creating a shared meeting agenda (see Figure 5.24).

When you are ready to share with an external audience, Plectica systems maps present ideas dynamically by walking through (often nonlinear) ideas in a linear, stepwise way. A stepwise walkthrough of the map can be built, much like a slide deck, but with the added benefits of:

• Showing the audience the structure of the ideas (how things are deconstructed, related, etc.)
• The audience sees individual ideas in their context
• The audience sees that this walkthrough of the map is one way to move through the ideas, but not the only way
• The presenter's ideas are shown to the audience in the same structure that the presenter thought them through, which allows the audience to deeply understand and push back in places where they disagree

It is widely accepted that presentation software such as PowerPoint, Keynote, and Google Slides (which share the same architecture) are designed for the presenter rather than the audience.[44,45] This is unfortunate, as a presentation should share ideas to help everyone build the same meaning, not merely

to see the same information. Presenting your work, systems, processes, or challenges to your colleagues through the visual representation of systems maps provides a great stepwise process for increased understanding of them and also puts this newfound clarity to use by aligning it with action steps, tasks, work assignments, and workflows (see OutDo).

Build knowledge across your organization through the use of existing content (canonical information) generated by other data sources or other maps. Along with a personal library of the ideas you create, the Plectica software has "stock libraries," such as Wikipedia, or add-on libraries, such as LexisNexis, accessible within the mapping canvas. These data can also be used to create new organizational libraries for canonical ideas (for example, your corporate vision or a specific airplane part with metadata that can be used in any map). These libraries of individual canonical ideas, map portions, maps, or sets of maps (atlases), which are searchable and reusable in any existing or new maps, save you time by not having to reinvent the wheel. This maximizes efficiency by making every idea, portion of a map, map, or atlas of maps reusable through accessible libraries.

Figure 5.25: Canonical ideas can be inserted into maps in situ

In addition, these reusable libraries can not only be found but also "forked," so you can utilize a canonical card or map but then adapt it for a slightly different purpose, and forks can be tracked internally to show the evolution of canonical cards or maps. This reusability, as well as the archival nature of the platform, means that all shared maps and map elements are available through search, providing what amounts to a large visual knowledge base. This knowledge base can be used in part or in its entirety to onboard new team members or new employees to the organization.

Likewise, portions of maps or entire maps can be converted into reusable templates or simply cut-and-pasted for reuse. And, cards within maps can be linked to other maps, creating an interconnected web of maps. Thus, there are many ways in which an individual or leader can share ideas within an organization: collaborative mapping, presentation, or using existing maps, content, or databases within maps to create an organizational knowledge base. While sharing seems like a basic idea, it has a profound effect on the degree to which organizational knowledge is built, communicated, refined, captured, and distributed to increase efficiencies and effectiveness.

Successful collaboration can be achieved from becoming a complex adaptive system, similar to a school of fish or flock of birds. As discussed earlier in this chapter, and in greater detail in Chapter 1, much can be learned and applied from the research of complex adaptive systems to facilitate collaboration in organizations. As we learned from Iain Couzin and his research on collective animal behavior, collaboration can best be achieved by identifying, understanding and applying the underlying simple rules all individuals in an organization should follow (or VMCL). Building collaborative maps in real-time can ensure all individual actors in your organization have a shared mental model of these simple rules, whether it is of a capacital function, mission, or vision, in order to learn and grow from each other and stay in sync. The result will be complex, emergent behavior, allowing you to OutDo your competition.

The Science of Collaboration and Swarm Intelligence

To understand the underpinnings of collaboration, you inevitably need to look to the power of swarm intelligence (SI). SI, a term coined by Gerardo Beni and Jing Wang in 1989, is the collective behavior of decentralized, self-organized systems. SI involves a population of individual agents acting locally, both with one another and with their environment.[46]

These agents, unaware of the global context, follow simple, local rules to bring about emergent, adaptive, and complex behavior. Iain Couzin's research on collective animal behavior at Princeton University demonstrated these underlying simple rules flocks were following, which led to their remarkable and emergent behavior. SI shows us that successful collaboration can come from identifying, understanding and applying the underlying simple rules all individuals in an organization should follow (VMCL).

Figure 5.26: Swarm behavior in a flock of birds

OutDo: Align Ideas to Action

Once your systems map has been built and improved to the point where you feel confident and clear about it (Out-Think), and shared (OutSync), it is time to align this new-found clarity with action steps, tasks, work assignments, and workflows (OutDo).

The importance of aligning our ideas to action is underscored by new understandings of human behavior and cognition. It turns out that action (what we do, how we do it, and how effective it is) is intimately tied to our mental model of the system in which we are acting. Therefore, we should think before, during, and after we take action. The action should be totally embedded in the context of a clear understanding of the system itself. In other words, you create individual and team tasks in context by using maps of your mental models to create and assign tasks and keep actions (how/what) closely aligned with purpose (why), thereby creating and assigning tasks based on your understanding of the system itself.

The importance of aligning our ideas to action is underscored by new understandings of human behavior and cognition. Action is intimately tied to our mental model of the system in which we are acting.

This means that the clarity of understanding that you've gained so far should directly translate to the to-do lists and workflows you create to get a job done. This is why it's important to create tasks and assignments directly out of the cards that are *already* part of your systems map. Let's revisit our earlier example of Alice Water and Chez Panisse to illustrate this point.

Farm to Table, Idea to Action

When designing the restaurant Chez Panisse, Alice Waters had an innovative vision for her restaurant that set it apart from others at the time. Alice re-imagined the way she sourced food for the restaurant. Importantly, this meant that due to Alice's unique mental model for what her restaurant would look like, the resulting actions she needed to take were wildly different from those of a neighboring restaurant (which would often rely on ready-made capacity from a food distributor). Unlike her competitors in other restaurants, Alice couldn't just pick up the phone and call a single distributor to order all of the necessary components on her menu. Instead, she needed to coordinate a complex series of actions in order to provide capacity to her restaurant; that is, to meet the mission that would fulfill the vision.

A systems map can help someone like Alice understand how to put new ideas into action. This systems map can first model Alice's ideas for Chez Panisse. Then, based on this model Alice can identify and map the necessary actions she would need to take to make these ideas become reality. Because the crux of Alice Waters' vision lies with re-thinking food procurement, Alice had to take countless steps to consider when and how much fish, fruits and vegetables, meats, grains, and other artisan products were available to realize her vision. For example, in Northern California, salmon is only available in May and August, and fishermen may only have a certain number of salmon available on any given day. Mapping her ideas and turning them into action would allow Alice to appropriately dictate how often she would need to perform certain tasks, helping her transition her visionary ideas to daily and weekly action lists (see Figure 5.27).

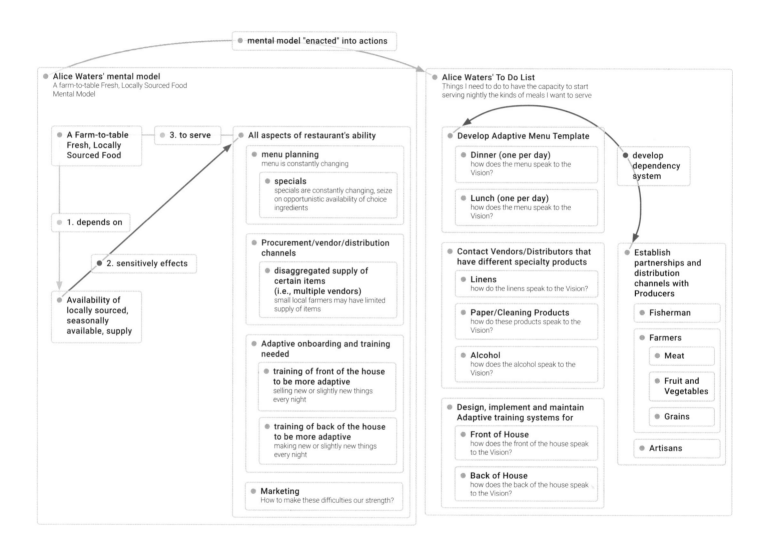

Figure 5.27: Enacting Alice Waters' ideas

In this way you can look at various cards associated with your work, systems, processes, or challenges and think about what the action items would be for each card. You can create as many action items per card as you wish. In addition, you can view these action items in place on the systems map, or in various other views (such as a list view, tasks you own or follow view, or team views). This simple idea ensures that *what* you do is never out of alignment or detached from *why* you are doing it.

The Science of How Schemas (mental models) Influence Behavior (action)

We know from science that mental models impact action. Schema (a generic term representing any model) summarize and are capable of describing, predicting and altering behavior. Thus, these models, whether they are cognitive or genetic (like a DNA sequence of an animal), are simply hypotheses that may or may not turn out to be true or viable. The behaviors, predictions and descriptions (or actions) that result from these models provide feedback based on real-world consequences and outcomes. Gell-Mann, through his analysis of complex adaptive systems, put thinking and learning (feedback) as the driver of a culture or organization's ability to adapt.[47] The survival of individuals and organizations alike depend on the ability to learn, and translate that learning into action. (See Figures 5.4 and 5.5 above for maps representing mental models that approximate the real world, and provide feedback to adapt our mental models.)

The survival of individuals and organizations alike depend on the ability to learn, and translate that learning into action.

OutLast: Beat the Competition

In our current VUCA world, organizations and their staff, need to be more adaptive to beat the competition. Collaboratively building and improving on your ideas (OutThink), sharing them (OutSync), and bringing your ideas to action (OutDo) can provide your organization with this adaptability, and allow you to outlast the competition.

The Science of Survival

From the study of nature and evolutionary biology, we know that the survival of the fittest does not mean the survival of the strongest or most brutish. Instead it means survival of the most adaptive. Microbiologists Lynn Margulis and Dorion Sagan said it best when they explained "Life did not take over the globe by combat, but by networking." By building and sharing mental models together, you can build a strong and adaptive network within your organization that can learn how to survive and thrive together, outlasting the competition.

CHECK 17 **We harness the power of mental models**

CHECK 18 **We train people to think in order to learn**

CHECK 19 **We constantly evolve our mental models**

Figure 5.28: Checks for creating a learning organization

CONCLUSION

Organizations will only succeed by learning: adapting to feedback from their external environment. As a leader, you can promote learning by demonstrating that learning is a priority to you. You are not just the leader, you are also the Chief Learning Officer. If you embrace learning, others will too. The ability of an organization to learn relies on creating a cadre of individuals who are robust, integrated thinkers.

Thinking is the process of structuring information to build meaning and act upon ideas. Systems thinkers innately check the distinctions they make, organize and reorganize ideas into part-whole systems, seek unidentified relationship among ideas, and purposefully analyse their ideas from multiple perspectives to gain deep understanding of concepts. Individual learning leads to organizational learning which leads to successful, collective action. In order to steer this collective action head-on to your vision, a system for capturing and distributing individual and organizational learning is paramount.

We must build teams that constantly seek feedback and embrace the evolution of their mental models towards greater excellence and performance. It is this simple tenet that underlies adaptation and survival of any organization. It is an essential piece of the DNA of any superorganism.

The power of building, sharing and evolving mental models can be harnessed, developed, and utilized to create a remarkable learning organization. As such, three ideas are paramount to success:

1. People need *tools* and *training* to help them think things through.
2. Thinking *fuels* learning.
3. Learning *drives* capacity, which makes mission possible and brings about vision.

At the ground level, build teams that are capable of mapping, sharing, and improving their ideas. These ideas, once they have survived interrogation via systems thinking, must then be acted upon. The true power of these steps—mapping, sharing, improving, and enacting ideas—creates a deep understanding of the system itself, the wider context in which our problems occur, and helps to identify key points in the system for translation into action to affect the change we seek. It is the connection among our mental models, our awareness of our own thinking, and the connection between thought and action that will ultimately lead to adaptability and success in an ever-changing, often volatile environment in which our organizations compete.

CHAPTER 6 LEADING A CULTURE SHIFT WITH VMCL

CHECK   1   Our vision depicts a desired future state

CHECK   2   Our vision is intrinsically motivating

CHECK   3   Our vision is short and simple

CHECK   4   We measure our vision

CHECK   5   We ensure our vision lives in hearts and minds

CHECK   6   Our mission is action(s) done repeatedly

CHECK   7   Our mission brings about our vision

CHECK   8   Our mission explains WHO does WHAT for WHOM

CHECK   9   Our mission is clear, concise, and easily understood

CHECK 10   We measure our mission

CHECK 11   We ensure our mission lives in hearts and minds

CHECK 12   We ensure that mission moments are sacrosanct

CHECK 13   We build capacity in order to do our mission

CHECK 14   We build capacity through a system of systems

CHECK 15   We map capacity to understand and better design systems

CHECK 16   We use learning to expand our capacity

CHECK 17   We harness the power of mental models

CHECK 18   We train people to think in order to learn

CHECK 19   We constantly evolve our mental models

CHECK 20   **We create a culture of vision, mission, capacity, and learning**

LEADING A CULTURE SHIFT WITH VMCL

Culture is a thousand things, a thousand times. It's living the core values when you hire; when you write an email; when you are working on a project; when you are walking in the hall.
—Brian Chesky, Founder, Airbnb[1]

Many thought leaders today are talking about company culture as if it's akin to capturing a unicorn. It carries a romantic and mythological appeal that makes it an irresistible topic of conversation, but they still haven't fully figured out how to effectively shape it to drive the right behaviors in their organizations.
—Chris Cancialosi[2]

Culture isn't just one aspect of the game—it IS the game.
—Lou Gerstner, former IBM CEO[3]

By this point, you have lovingly crafted your vision and mission, and given shape to your systems for capacity and learning. Congratulations! Your final task is to ensure that all of this lives in the hearts and the minds of your team. Remember:

• The vision and mission statements you create are mental models—they have meaning beyond the words used to describe them. (This goes for your capacity maps and learning systems, as well.)

• Mental models must be shared—and by "shared" we don't mean sent in an email. We mean held in common. Shared in their meaning.

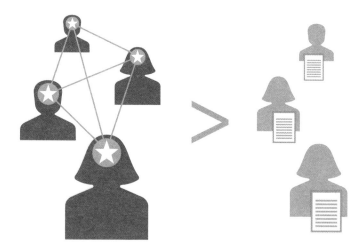

FIGURE 6.1: Mental models; shared and unshared

Thinking → Learning → Organizational
Learning → Capacity → Mission → Vision

Thinking drives learning. In turn, learning drives capacity, which serves mission and brings about vision. As we described

1. A mental model is made up of information and thinking and thinking follows the four patterns of DSRP. This is written as

$$m = i + t\{DSRP\}$$

2. Individual learning is a change in a mental model; written as

$$L_{ind} = \triangle m$$

3. Organizational learning is a change in a mental model shared by the agents (A) in your organization (which could be individual employees, teams, groups, etc.); written as

$$L_{org} = (\triangle m)A$$

4. Organizational culture, which sometimes feels amorphous, is similar but different from organizational learning. It can be defined as mental models shared by agents. It is written as

$$C_{org} = mA$$

So how do you enculturate the mental models that are so important to making your business thrive? You must ensure that every employee, team leader, partner, and even customer has a shared definition, meaning, and passion for the mental models that drive your organization. In addition, as these mental models evolve, so too does the sharing of this evolution, so that your organization is ever-adaptive and evergreen.

CULTURE IS NOT MYSTERIOUS OR AMORPHOUS

CULTURE IS SHARED MENTAL MODELS

VMCL Will Not Implement Itself

Plato said, "Well begun is half done." Of the 20 checkpoints on the VMCL checklist, some are things you do once and then revisit occasionally when they are no longer serving you. Checks 1, 2, 3, 6, 7, 8, and 9 guide your work when you are designing your vision and mission and should be revisited whenever necessary. Once you are able to check these off, you are 50% done, and officially at the end of the beginning.

But then there's the other 50%: implementation. VMCL is immensely powerful and can do a lot of things for your organization. But one of the things it can't do is implement itself. The final check on your list is the work of implementation.

Check #20 is really a check to make sure that you implement all the other checks (the ones in dark blue) in Figure 6.1.

Take Check #5 (We ensure our vision lives in hearts and minds) and Check #11 (We ensure our mission lives in hearts and minds), for example. You read about the importance of these in previous chapters, but now you have to do it. You have to make sure that the vision and mission, like a cute puppy, begins to warm the hearts of your employees. And Check #4 (We measure our vision) and Check #10 (We measure our mission) mean that now you have to inculcate metrics and make them visible in your organizational culture.

People need to know that this is how the organization is measuring success! You'll also want to be sure that Check #12 (We ensure that mission moments are sacrosanct) is enculturated by spot-checking if there is a deep and abiding reverence for mission moments. You will constantly keep an eye on capacital systems (and get others to watch, as well) to ensure that they are up to snuff. You can use Check #13 through Check #16 to help guide you.

And you will want to ensure that learning is alive and well with the help of Check #17 through Check #19.

The final check (#20)—the focus of this chapter—is not for vision, mission, capacity, or learning individually, but for VMCL as a whole. It's a final check that ensures you are implementing the other checks. This chapter will show you how to do that via many practical examples. So, let's dive into the last and most important check of all.

Do this in your culture everyday

Build a VMCL Culture

CHECK	4	**We measure our vision**
CHECK	5	**We ensure our vision lives in hearts and minds**
CHECK	10	**We measure our mission**
CHECK	11	**We ensure our mission lives in hearts and minds**
CHECK	12	**We ensure that mission moments are sacrosanct**
CHECK	13	**We build capacity in order to do our mission**
CHECK	14	**We build capacity through a system of systems**
CHECK	15	**We map capacity to understand and better design systems**
CHECK	16	**We use learning to expand our capacity**
CHECK	17	**We harness the power of mental models**
CHECK	18	**We train people to think in order to learn**
CHECK	19	**We constantly evolve our mental models**
CHECK	20	We create a culture of vision, mission, capacity, and learning

Figure 6.2: Using the checklist to lead and build a VMCL culture

Check #20: We create a culture of vision, mission, capacity, and learning

Leaders often say their most powerful asset is their people. We disagree. People in and of themselves aren't that powerful, especially if they are bickering, at cross purposes, or ignoring one another. People who share common mental models are powerful. **Culture** is what happens when *people share mental models*.[4] Culture isn't some mysterious thing that only happens if we're lucky. All groups have culture: culture occurs and evolves naturally. Perhaps most important, culture can be built.[5]

For a mental model to be shared it must be (1) understood the same way by everyone in the group, and (2) believed in and endorsed by the group. To say it another way, when mental models are shared—that is, *understood and embraced in the same way*—among members of an organization, they constitute organizational culture. Therefore, each mental model—for example, Quality is Job One—must mean the same thing to and resonate with all group members. This is why organizations are best served by concise and unambiguous statements of their vision, mission, and values. (In other words, room for interpretation is destructive!)

So, how shared must a mental model be for it to be considered part of organizational culture? At the individual level, there will always be variation in how deeply understood and ingrained any mental model is. It is unlikely that even the most persuasive leader can perfectly inculcate their vision and mission, let alone myriad other mental models of import to organizational function, among everyone. One employee may intellectually support the mission but it may lack emotional resonance and hence inspirational power for him. So variation in adoption and adherence to mental models is the norm. Certainly it is normal and in some cases might be beneficial to have variation in many of the less consequential parts of one's organizational culture (e.g., how to run a meeting).

The key is that your most important mental models must be understood and jointly held in the hearts and minds of the group. The strength of a company's culture is a function of how widespread and deeply ingrained those mental models are. Deeply ingrained mental models, in turn, should drive behavior, both directly and indirectly.[6]

Your organization's vision and mission and your core values (if you have them)—these are not just statements and lists, they are mental models that need to be built by everyone in the organization. If you want to build culture, build and share your mental models. There are numerous words that are roughly synonymous to culture, including: ideology, climate, values, beliefs, traditions, and norms. If you are wed to using one of these words to talk about your company, you needn't despair.

All those things are mental models that, when shared among group members, constitute organizational culture.

Core Tenets of Organizational Culture

Members of your organization will share a large number of mental models, all of varying importance and centrality to the organization and its success. So what are the most important mental models—the pillars of your culture? Where do you focus first and foremost? Organizational success depends on sharing the right mental models, ones that are complexity-friendly and promote learning and adaptation.

The single most important mental model of any organization is its **vision**—the desired goal or future state the organization seeks (its *raison d'être*). CEO and author of *Fueled by Failure*, Jeremy Bloom, offers the following first step for creating a strong culture: "Establishing a culture you believe in means having a clear and consistent vision and knowing how you'd like everyone, inside and outside, to view the company." Steve Howe of EY explained: "To improve its culture, a company must first define its purpose: why does it exist, and what greater good does it serve?"[7] So the mental model you must first inculcate is your vision.

Inextricably linked to that is the **mission**—the steps you repeat to achieve the vision. We can't emphasize enough how important it is for people to know what they must do and why they are doing it (that is, to what end)! As UK psychology professor Steve Taylor writes, *"The need for purpose is one of the defining characteristics of human beings. Human beings crave purpose, and suffer serious psychological difficulties when we don't have it. Purpose is a fundamental component of a fulfilling life."*[8]

Another way to think about culture is as a mechanism to purposefully leverage the four natural functions—vision, mission, capacity, learning—of any organization.

All **capacity** systems in your organization should be geared toward executing the mission (to achieve the vision); there should be shared understandings around capacity, as well. What does this entail? It is vital that every single member of your organization understands

- The major capacity systems of the organization, including their purpose (to fulfill the mission to achieve the vision)
- How the systems fit together (align) to form a system of systems
- How he or she contributes to capacity (i.e., what her or his role is in the different capacity systems)

Finally, the **learning** function must also be encultrated, so that the organization's mental models can be updated to reflect reality and facilitate adaptation to internal and external conditions and events.

Culture with Consequences

By definition, all groups (including organizational members) are characterized by culture(s). If your articulated company culture—its set of key mental models—is not having the anticipated behavioral consequences, that's a sign that it fails to reflect the content and/or complexity of your actual culture. Advising leaders to start with "a realistic recognition of the culture's current status," organizational change experts Jon Katzenbach and DeAnne Aguirre note that culture is embedded in mindsets and demonstrated behaviorally.[9]

> If your articulated company culture—its set of key mental models—is not having the anticipated behavioral consequences, that's a sign that it fails to reflect the content and/or complexity of your actual culture.

Indeed, much of culture is reflected in behavioral norms[10], and it is not unusual for workplace norms to outright contradict formal written rules or articulated corporate statements of culture. If that is the case, you need to figure out what your current (dominant) organizational culture is by seeing how the complex adaptive system of your organization behaves. And, of course, you will likely find that your organization, if sufficiently large, has subcultures. Regardless, ask yourself what simple rules (mental models) the agents follow.

Figure 6.3: Unwritten rules[11]

It's absolutely critical that the key tenets of your culture—written on your website or perhaps featured prominently on an office wall, and promoted internally and externally—are in fact shared mental models; meaning that they are deeply understood and held dear by everyone in the organization. The dissonance produced by proclaiming one culture while possessing or even fostering another is bad for morale, to say the least. As one expert put it, "Empty values statements (articulated mental models that are *not* shared) create cynical and dispirited employees, alienate customers, and undermine managerial credibility."[12]

This concern can be seen in the frequent emphasis by CEOs of top-rated workplaces on *authenticity* and "walking the talk." Take Zappos, which is now in the business of teaching other companies about culture. CEO Tony Hsieh explained:

> We believe that it's really important to come up with core values that you can commit to. And by commit, we mean that you're willing to hire and fire based on them. If you're willing to do that, then you're well on your way to building a company culture that is in line with the brand you want to build.[13]

Facebook's Sheryl Sandberg wisely advised, "True leadership stems from individuality that is honestly and sometimes imperfectly expressed... Leaders should strive for authenticity over perfection."[14] Starbucks CEO Howard Schultz expressed a similar idea about brands "built from the heart": "Their foundations are stronger because they are built with the strength of the human spirit, not an ad campaign. The companies that are lasting are those that are authentic."[15]

It's absolutely critical that the key tenets of your culture are in fact shared mental models; meaning that they are deeply understood and held dear by everyone in the organization.

Ron Ashkenas, Partner Emeritus of Schaffer Consulting, opined, "Put teeth into the new culture by integrating it into HR processes. People tend to do what's measured and rewarded. ... Use the desired behaviors as criteria for hiring, promoting, rewarding, and developing people."[16] He gives the example of Jack Welch's transformation of GE, which was marked by the public firing of leaders who, although they achieved exceptionally high earnings, failed to demonstrate the behaviors prescribed by the new GE culture.

There are many mental models, of varying importance, that organizational members share. Leaders would be well-advised to jettison or at least reconsider articulated aspects of culture that lack the predicted behavioral consequences—that don't drive members to support the vision, fulfill the mission, build capacity, or engage in learning. Save your efforts for teaching, inculcating, and inspiring your team with what's important.

"I don't know how it started, either. All I know is that it's part of our corporate culture."

Figure 6.4: The origin of dress codes in corporate culture[17]

Old or New, Organizational Culture Must Be Built

All this talk of culture is of course useless if it's not implemented. Noting how difficult culture is to define and pinpoint for executives, Chris Cancialosi, Partner and Founder of gothamCulture, nonetheless argues

> Just because I don't understand astrophysics doesn't mean it's not real or that it doesn't impact my day-to-day life. The difference between astrophysics and culture is that you have the ability to influence your organization's culture.[18]

Culture can feel amorphous, like a cloud. Hard to pin down or define. And to some extent it is. The scientific term for this is dissipative structure: a structure that is constantly changing while maintaining a recognizable steady state. So, when you see a cloud in the sky, it isn't a fixed thing. The air molecules are constantly changing, but the cloud-like shape is maintained. A cloud is an area of "cloudiness" and the molecules that make it up are constantly entering and exiting, yet the cloud form maintains itself. Think of your culture this way, too. While you may have employees, customers, and partners coming and going at various times and rates, the culture of the organization somehow persists. Where culture is concerned, this persistence of form is due to the sharing and diffusion of the mental models.

So how do we build culture? What is the process? Well, it's no small feat. To create an effective organization, we must do the hard work of getting people to share the same mental models. We need to identify what these mental models are, make them crystal clear and simple, and have a way to know whether people understand them. The alternative is that you have a bunch of people who share superficial attributes, such as where they work or what it says on their pay stub. That won't translate into a commitment to a larger cause, a passion for work, or a consistently positive customer experience.

To create an effective organization, we must do the hard work of getting people to share the same mental models.

The process of building culture is, by and large, the same for both new organizations and for organizations seeking culture change, because whether you have new or seasoned employees, a new mental model must be learned and internalized. Nonetheless, there are of course some salient differences when faced with an established culture. First, in a new organization, you will have to contend with a group characterized by different mental models and thus acclimated to different behaviors.

With an established organization, you may face an entrenched culture characterized by a group with shared understanding and allegiance to particular ways of thinking and behaving. This unity of mental models requires a more intense, sustained, and systematic process of culture building. This can be seen in the fact that approximately 70% of all organizational change initiatives fail.[19] That said, whether faced with relatively unified or disparate mental models among a team, every leader must build culture by sharing new mental models. Here's how.

Learning Often Starts with *Unlearning*

Remember that all organizations, new and old, have cultures. They will vary in the degree to which everyone shares your organization's key mental models. In the case of established organizations, culture is likely rather entrenched and has a taken-for-granted quality. So the first step in these types of situations may be teaching organization members how to unlearn old mental models. This process should start by analysis of the simple rules employees follow that produce the emergent property of organizational behavior.

	Simple Rules	lead to...	Emergent Behavior *What do we actually see?*
Sample	Examples: • Junior staff work long hours • Junior staff rarely speak to one another • Senior staff spend most of each day in meetings with one another	*leads to...*	Example: Lower level employees are highly competitive to get the attention of senior level staff. Work is siloed. Our culture rewards competition over collaboration.
Current State (Your turn)		*leads to...*	
Future State (Work backward start with the emergent behavior you want to see)		*leads to...*	

Activity 6.1: Emergent organizational behavior

Discuss as a group what the true organizational purpose appears to be, and what the simple steps are, the mission, that people routinely take to move closer to that vision. What are the major capacity systems and do they align with the mission? In other words, do different departments and initiatives and work teams and projects help the organization do the mission to achieve the vision? Finally, what is the role of learning in the organization, and it is also aligned with the other functions of VMCL? We strongly recommend diagramming the actual, existing VMCL of your organization (including noting disagreement or factions when they exist) before building your new VMCL. We love the following statement by Facebook software engineer Pierre Raynaud, as it exemplifies the importance (and difficulty) of unlearning.

> Innovation can be crippled, as new ideas are expected to come from the individuals who are least likely to generate truly new ideas (because they're so deeply involved in and biased by the details of the current design and implementation), and these individuals are given implicit or explicit authority to dwarf disruptive ideas from the outside.[20]

Whether faced with relatively unified or disparate mental models among a team, every leader must build culture by sharing new mental models

Unlearning can sometimes best be achieved in immersive experiences. Zappos, for example, uses this process for new employees: "It's a four-week training program, in which we go over company history, the importance of customer service, the long-term vision of the company, our philosophy about company culture and then you're actually on the phone for two weeks, taking calls from customers."[21]

	Vision *What is the true organizational purpose?*	**Mission** *What are the simple rules we follow to move closer to vision?*	**Capacity** *What are the capacital systems? Do they align with mission?*	**Learning** *What is the role of learning? Is this in alignment with V, M, and C?*
Sample	Example: A world without fleas.	Evangelize. Educate. Empower.	**First-Order Systems** • Sales & marketing • Training development • Engineering, (R & D) **Second-Order Systems** • Purchasing • Human talent • Accounting & finance	• Acme knowledge base • Acme onboarding of new employees/partners/contractors • Acme training and tools (to question, test, and improve VMCL)
Current State				
Future State				

Activity 6.2: Unlearning your current VMCL

Culture Campaigns and Modeling Culture

Deep understanding comes over time, and is demonstrated and embodied in behavior. Every conversation and every interaction is an opportunity to build culture. Mental models should be shared through the social (ideally organization-wide) use of icons, slogans, ceremonies, rituals, and other reifications (i.e., ideas made tangible). These are all instances of culture that help inculcate meaning—they make tangible the mental model you need understood.

Deep understanding comes over time, and is demonstrated and embodied in behavior. Every conversation and every interaction is an opportunity to build culture.

Given the increasing tendency of organizations to post statements characterizing themselves and what they do, it is vital to emphasize that *words alone mean nothing* if they do not represent shared mental models, woven into the hearts and minds of your people. They are the fabric of your organization. They are your culture. Hence, you need to create a culture campaign to enculturate your vision and mission. If you don't do this, you've wasted your time—you'll be left with words on a page that do nothing to shape employees' behaviors. A culture campaign is internal, but resembles the external marketing campaigns we all know.

Many of you probably know of the "Think Different" campaign of Apple. Interestingly, the campaign's purpose and origin was internal before it was made available for public consumption. Scott Goodson explains how Steve Jobs sought to revitalize the company upon his return in the 1990s.

One of the first things Jobs did was to start a "Think Different" movement inside the company, particularly aimed at the product developers. Before the outside world ever saw those famous "Think Different" ads, those two words were appearing on banners and T-shirts at the company's headquarters, ensuring that everyone at the company lived and breathed this philosophy. "Steve was inviting everybody in that company to rethink everything," recalls the longtime Apple ad chief, Lee Clow of TBWA/Chiat/Day. "At the time, he didn't have any new product yet, and Apple was almost out of business. But to him, the first mission was to get everybody singing off the same song sheet again." By the time "Think Different" became a public campaign—and an external movement that rallied creative people everywhere around this idea—it was already an established internal movement at Apple.[22]

Chief marketing officers (CMOs) are typically tasked with creating external marketing for a company's products and brand. However, CMOs are increasingly being asked to use their marketing skills *within* a company to improve corporate culture.

Experts attribute this trend to more consumers deciding to avoid companies they distrust or whose actions and policies they dislike.[23] Hubspot and Zappos are two companies that have conducted successful and intensive culture campaigns. Be sure to check out Hubspot's 128-page slide deck on their culture code, available on their website and LinkedIn.

Beyond creating a culture campaign, there is a simple yet profound way that leaders must promote their company's culture. As The Clemmer Group advises, "The single biggest key to transforming an organization's culture starts with executives defining and developing their own behaviors. This must then cascade down the entire organization."[24] Business author Scott Berkun writes, "Every CEO is in fact a Chief Cultural Officer. The terrifying thing is it's the CEO's actual behavior, not their speeches or the list of values they have put up on posters, that defines what the culture is."[25]

It's a cliché for a reason: actions speak louder than words. Katzenbach and Aguirre explain:

> Recognizing the importance of culture in business is not the same thing as being an effective cultural chief executive. The CEO is the most visible leader in a company. His or her direct engagement in all facets of the company's culture can make an enormous difference, not just in how people feel about the company, but in how they perform.[26]

We highly recommend the well-tested leadership practice of walking around.[27] Local action (simple rules followed by individuals) leads to the emergent properties you want in your organization. So walk around and observe the culture in action, teach it, model it, enact it. In his second book, *A Passion for Excellence*, influential thought leader Tom Peters endorsed "managing by wandering about" as the foundation of leadership and excellence, and advised that leaders should:

- Listen to what people are saying
- Use the opportunity to transmit the company's values face to face
- Be prepared and able to give people help on the spot.[28]

As Airbnb founder Brian Chesky opined: "Culture is a thousand things, a thousand times. It's living the core values when you hire; when you write an email; when you are working on a project; when you are walking in the hall."[29]

Leading Organizational Change Is a Culture-Building Campaign

Quick pop quiz! Organizational change is:
  A. Easy
  B. Hard

If you answered A, you either work in an organization composed of 1 person, have never tried organizational change, or are an organizational genius and need not read any further. If, like most of us, you answered B, here's why: command hierarchies don't actually work as promised. If they did, controlling organizational behavior would be easy. All you'd have to do is decide at the top how things should be and then pass it down the hierarchical chain. At each level of hierarchy each person would do exactly what their boss wanted and presto! We'd have the desired organizational outcome!

McKinsey reports that 70% of change efforts fail, largely because of employee resistance and lack of management support.[30] But guess what: half the battle of organizational change is cultural change. In fact, we'd venture so far as to say that it is impossible to meaningfully change an organization without changing its culture, its shared mental models.[31]

The reality is that most folks reading this book do not have the luxury of setting direction for a startup organization, and therefore must be concerned with the issue of changing a pre-existing culture. Even in new organizations, leaders will have to contend with diverse pre-existing mental models (biases) of its employees. A recent article described the approach many CEOs take when confronted with the need to change their company's culture.

> They turn up the volume on the inspirational messages. They raise the bar and set stretch goals with new statements of the vision, mission, values, and purpose of the company. They bear down on costs and castigate people for complacency.[32]

Alternatively, they delegate the task to experts. Either way, these approaches are rarely successful. And while things like company slogans and logos can be changed easily, the deeper elements of culture take much more time and effort to build and alter.

Katzenbach and Aguirre offer sage advice about cultural (organizational) change.

> Demonstrate positive urgency by focusing on your company's aspirations—its unfulfilled potential—rather than on any impending crisis. Pick a critical few behaviors that exemplify the best of your company and culture, and that you want everyone to adopt. Set an example by visibly adopting a couple of these behaviors yourself. Balance your appeals to the company to include both rational and emotional cues. Make the change sustainable by maintaining vigilance on the few critical elements that you have established as important. In all this activity, avoid delegating your culture-oriented actions. Do as much as you can yourself.[33]

Another critical task is to visually and behaviorally represent (rather than just verbally articulate) the core tenets of the old culture and the new mental models that will take their place. This unlearning process is the definition of leadership—taking people from the undesirable or suboptimal present to the desired future state (i.e., the vision).

Your Organization Is a Network, So Choose a Suitable Change Model

The network structure underlying groups and organizations of all types is conducive to a systems approach based on complexity science. This is because collectives of individuals, no matter how structured, are complex adaptive systems.

Irrespective of their formal structure—rigid formalized hierarchy, fluid and minimalist structure, or somewhere in between—all organizations are made up of the networked interactions of individuals (agents) who adapt to and learn from an environment. All organizational structures are overlaid on a network of semi-autonomous individuals. In short, VMCL provides a model that corresponds with all organizations—formally structured or not—because it focuses on their underlying structure and network behavior.

Network theorists have contributed substantially to our understanding of social change, influence, and contagion processes—all of which are germane to culture building. A recent study demonstrated that a small group of diehard proponents of an idea or position—just 10% of a population—can sway the majority of society who hold a contrary opinion but are open to other views.[34] The 10% represents a tipping point after which society rapidly converts to the new mental model, and this occurs across several different network structures. Other work on collective action emphasizes that considerable change is often achieved in groups by just 5% of members.[35] Building on these insights and recognizing the inherent difficulty of changing hearts and minds, our model focuses less on achieving immediate group-wide adoption and instead offers a process for incrementally building support for a culture. This change effort—the process by which mental models are spread organization-wide—is best represented and tracked by a culture-building graph (CBG).

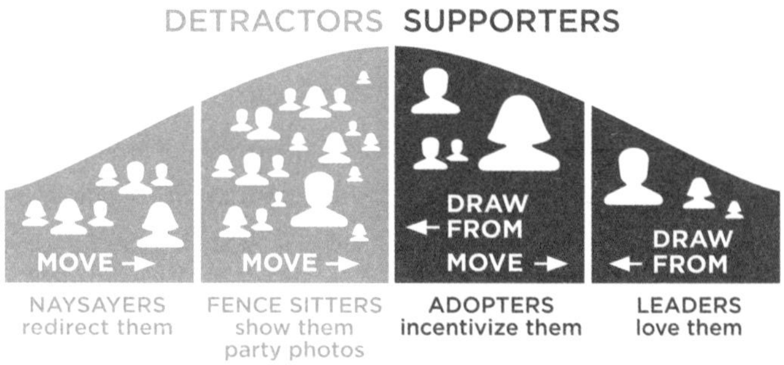

Figure 6.5: Culture-building graph

A CBG is a tool for organizational change that demarcates who is on board with the organization's key mental models and who is not (and to what degree). While the distribution of support in your organization is unlikely to fit a bell curve, you can often expect a smaller number of ardent opponents ("naysayers") and ardent proponents ("leaders") of organizational culture.

Remember the CBG is not a compliance model, it's an indication of your progress in inculcating culture; that is, your progress in teaching (indeed, selling) mental models. CBGs help identify work that needs to be done to make the shift toward a new organizational culture. CBGs can be used in the same way that a Senate Majority Leader might place images of senators in the Yay or Nay column in preparation for a vote. Placing individual employees on the CBG helps leaders know where the work needs to be done and how to adequately teach, motivate, and incentivize each individual. Incentives, of course, needn't be monetary; in fact, they are ideally intrinsic (hence your job as chief culture officer/mental model builder for your team). As Visa credit card founder and CEO Dee Hock wrote, "Money motivates neither the best people nor the best in people. It can move the body and influence the mind, but it cannot touch the heart or move the spirit; that is reserved for belief, principle, and morality."[36] And remember that the formal title and position of an employee says little about where they reside on the CBG. The Clemmer Group asks in a blog: "Are vision, mission, or values just words from above or do they vibrantly live in all key people decisions like hiring, promotions/succession planning, recognition/appreciation/celebration practices, and tough actions like discipline or letting someone go?" Your lower-level leaders are likely to vary in their support for and implementation of your culture. "Departmental or division managers can shape their culture (leading), sit back and wait for direction from above (following), or throw up their hands in frustration at executives' lack of culture leadership (wallowing)."[37]

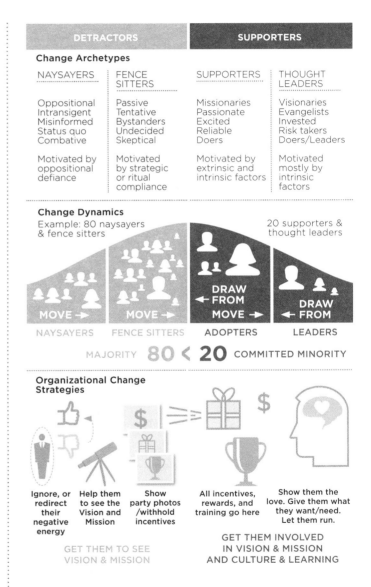

FIGURE 6.6: Culture-building graph archetype strategies

Remember the CBG is not a compliance model, it's an indication of your progress in inculcating culture; that is, your progress in teaching (indeed, selling) mental models. CBGs help identify work that needs to be done to make the shift toward a new organizational culture.

Leading Each CBG Group

On the right side of the CBG are culture adopters and leaders. These folks support cultural pillars. On the left side of the graph are nonsupporters: fence sitters and naysayers. The idea is to manage the process of getting as many people as possible from the left to the right side of the graph, thereby creating a critical mass of support. As one might imagine, culture leaders in the organization typically don't need much more than camaraderie and appreciation to continue their work advocating the culture. We generally give them love and support. We enlist them as cultural ambassadors and hold them up as examples. You do not need very many senior leaders to start a few critical behaviors rolling through the company. As Katzenbach and Aguirre suggest:

Get several well-known executives to step away from the norms of the past with you. People throughout the work-

force will rapidly take notice and do the same, creating an atmosphere of approval and support. In short, by seeking out other early adopters of these behaviors, and working with them directly to sharpen their influence and deploy it more effectively, you will gain far more leverage as a cultural leader.[38]

The majority of those who buy into the culture can be called adopters, and this group is where your incentives and rewards should go to effect change. While they exhibit compliance, can you discern the source? Is it ritual/habitual? Strategic and therefore more precarious? Or do the adopters embrace the organization's key mental models? Obviously, this begins with ensuring deep understanding among group members of the VMCL. But to be clear: this is where you focus most of your time and other resources.

Let's talk about the left side of the graph, the two groups that are not fully on board. Ironically, while adopters are the proper target of your resources, we will devote more ink to nonsupporters. Organizational leaders often make the mistake of rewarding fence sitters to entice them to move to the right (toward cultural leader), which ironically only serves to motivate fence sitting. Fence sitters are waiting to see what's going to happen, so you want to avoid rewarding this behavior. But you also want to teach them and show them the benefits of joining the culture. Do this by showing them what we call "party photos"—assorted communication through various media that convey to fence sitters that the side of corporate company culture is the place to be—they'll get rewards, have fun, have a sense of purpose and belonging, and love what they're doing. Resist giving fence sitters any rewards, show them party photos, and scrupulously avoid getting in control battles with them.

Organizational leaders often make the mistake of rewarding fence sitters to entice them to move to the right (toward cultural leader), which ironically only serves to motivate fence sitting.

Naysayers, a veritable fact of life for new leaders or reformers, require a different strategy. They can be a heterogeneous group, so the first step is to learn their grievances, as they may have very legitimate complaints. In some instances, you can move naysayers to become culture proponents. Other times leaders may simply confront staunch opposition to change. In such instances, they should focus on redirecting the naysayers' energy and not letting them set the agenda with their opposition. Having earnestly entertained their grievances, leadership must refocus its efforts on other group members.

Do not simultaneously discuss mission, capacity, and learning with naysayers. Focus first and foremost on the vision. Why? The organizational vision is often less controversial than the tactical and strategic considerations that come with deciding mission, capacity, and learning for an organization. Say you lead a company that makes products that facilitate environmentally friendly behavior on the part of consumers. As a group, you come up with a tentative vision of "Doubling recycling and composting in metropolitan areas." You want to do this through a mission—admittedly loosely defined—of "Making it easy to do the right thing." Your leadership team is instituting plans for capacity and learning and identifying key mental models that will constitute culture while ensuring the alignment of your VMCL.

You face a small but vociferous cadre of naysayers. So you focus on the vision: "Are you against doubling rates of recycling and composting?" If the answer is no, we know there's a chance we can move them toward being cultural proponents. If the answer is yes, then it becomes clear that the naysayer (1) is a poor fit for the organization, (2) has some relevant and important position that should be considered, and/or (3) may adhere to their opposition no matter what you do. Anyway, once agreement is achieved on vision, discussion can move to mission (repeated steps to achieve the vision). If agreement is achieved there, discussion can proceed to culture/capacity and, eventually, to learning. Effective leadership moves incrementally toward building understanding, support of, and adherence to shared mental models; that is, it shifts the group to the right of the CBG.

With time and perseverance, you may succeed in building a cult-like culture. The word "cult" is not without negative associations, but hear us out. Cultures become cult-like when a vast majority of the organization fervently believes in and is passionate about the organization's key mental models. Research and management guru Jim Collins explains that organizations become great when they face the brutal realities of their business and build a focused culture.[39] He calls these cultures "cult-like" because they have a rigidly enforced set of cultural norms (even if the norms themselves are flexible). In other words, those individuals who don't fit, don't want to be there, and those people who do fit, love it. As an organizational leader, it's your job to build this cult-like culture by teaching and inculcating your key mental models.

We do not mean to suggest or recommend the creation of blind, unquestioning adherents. Stash Tea Company's Vice President of Operations argues that in building culture, "leaders need to engage employees in a way that solicits open, honest and creative feedback."[40] That's why a culture with learning (testing mental models against outside feedback) as a key tenet is so important.

One culture consultant argues that you can overemphasize cultural fitness, making it difficult to:

> ...hire and welcome employees who are different than the prevailing culture, even if they'd be an asset and great counterbalance at your company. Your company culture needs adjustment if it causes you to end up with a homogenized team who think and act the same.[41]

Google, undoubtedly one of the most successful organizations to date, has coined the term "Googleyness" to mean cultural fit. Their CEO says that what they look for is people who are *different* because "diversity leads to great ideas." He expounds by saying that cultural fit is more important than knowing how to do your job because if you fit the central tenets of their culture (humility and care for the environment of Google), you'll figure your job out over time.[42]

Inculcate VMCL Top-down and Bottom-up

In particular, we want to show you the power of enculturation of VMCL across scale. What we mean by this is that VMCL is a *fractal* in your organization. A fractal is a self-repeating structure or pattern—one that repeats at a very small scale, a medium scale, and a large scale. For the purpose of showing you this repeating pattern of VMCL, we want to break your organization into three distinct scalar groups:

1. The organization as a whole
2. The team level
3. The individual level

You could of course look at other levels of scale, like the departmental or project level, or even the single human thought level. We will leave those to your imagination for now and focus on the three above.

The Organizational Scale

At the organizational scale VMCL provides an overarching framework, the simple rules that govern all human interactions and behavior, if they are enculturated. To do this you need to make sure that VMCL isn't something you hang on a wall but integrate into the customs and icons of the organization. VMCL can play out in your logo and in the stories you tell. It can be used at the start of every meeting or to begin an all hands talk. CEOs often have a mini VMCL deck of a few slides that they present at the front of every talk they give to the organization. In can be embedded in your awards and in your mascot, in the customs and symbols of your organization. We've seen VMCL organizations cover their entire front entrance in elements of their VMCL.

Figure 6.7: Xactly Corporation's vision is front and center, literally, when you walk in the building

More important, your vision and mission metrics, the ones you painstakingly considered for each element, should be the measures and metrics that your employees live and breath by. They should be front and center. They should be more important than your stock price. They are the metrics associated with how you determine if you are getting the job done. One of the first things every company should do after affirming their own VMCL is to identify their vision-mission metrics and enculturate them as part of their administrative position, and as what frames their assessment of the health of their growing business. For example, the Acme Extermination Company's vision-mission metrics might look like this:

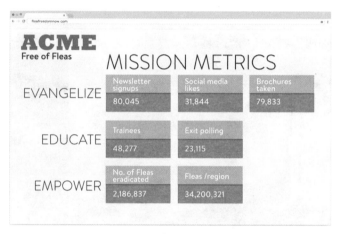

Figure 6.8: Mission isn't merely a statement, it is a call to action and a measurable indicator of success

If you have an intranet, a blog, or any other internal system, consider how you can get your vision-mission front and center in your organization's consciousness. But even that is not enough. Many CEOs, excited with the newfound clarity that VMCL work has brought them, ask us, "Now what should I do with this?" Our answer is, practice leadership by walking around. Walk around your offices, warehouses, or factories and talk directly to your employees about the vision and the mission. View these talks as user sessions (remember the internal product you are selling and marketing is VMCL). Find out what people really think about your vision-mission. Learn what they understand it, how they understand it, and what they don't. If you discover that there is a common misconception that people have about it, find a good story, metaphor, or other way of describing it better and make a concerted effort to undo the misconception. And find ways to incentivize and reward (often in subtle and informal ways) when people to "get it" or when they demonstrate "living it."

Use Maps

You might feel like you have a good understanding of the "big picture" of your organization, but your employees often do not. Sharing your map with them is critically important. It gives them a sense of purpose and place. It allows them to know where and how they fit into the bigger picture. It gives them context and grounding. And it fosters a culture of transparency. Let them participate in, or at least see, the evergreen and evolutionary nature of these maps. Get them used to change by making change incremental and constant. As the organization learns, its mental models change. In our research lab, we designed Plectica maps for this very purpose—to share mental models and, more important, to share how they are changing over time.

A VMCL map can be an indispensable tool for your organization, your leadership, your employees, and for onboarding new employees and partners.

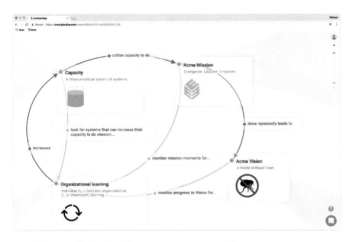

Figure 6.9: Getting everyone on the same page, literally, with a VMCL map

Note that there are numerous maps that are nested inside this larger scale map. These submaps are used at lower levels of scale in the organization.

The Team Scale

At team scale, VMCL plays out in important ways. Many team leaders find that the organizational vision-mission suffices for their team-level focus. But others (especially in larger organizations where the team level might be a department or large project) find it useful to create a team-level vision-mission that nests inside of the organizational vision-mission. Either way, all of the practices outline above at the organizational level can be carried out by team leaders (e.g., leadership by walking around, starting meetings with vision-mission, etc). But at the team level we see a lot more on the culture and learning parts of the spectrum. At the team level, people may be struggling with ineffective processes or systems and looking for ways to better understand or design these systems. Process level frameworks like objectives and key results, Agile Sprints, KanBan, or others are used or modified to increase teamwork. Often these existing frameworks need to be modified or customized to the unique needs of the team. This customization process takes the form of new maps that can be nested inside of larger organizational maps.

Teams often organize their work into manageable chunks (daily, weekly, monthly, quarterly) which are directed toward the company vision. Figure 6.9 shows a map of a team's Sprint planning, which should be seen as an expanded view of one piece of an organization's capacity map. This, by the way, is a simple illustration of how we can use maps to turn ideas into action and even to assign due dates and task assignments.

Figure 6.10: Agile Sprint map at the team level

The Individual Scale

At the individual scale VMCL plays itself out primarily in learning. That's not to say that vision, mission, and capacity are not ever present, but each employee's grasp of how they contribute to mental models is the best mechanism for deeply understanding himself or herself and the work. Additionally, developing an openness to seeing other's mental models, and a willingness to adapt is the foundation to functional teams that will have the impetus and the space to be creative, innovative, and disruptive in their thinking. It is these teams upon which organizational culture, values, and, ultimately, adaptability and success is built.

CONCLUSION

By now, we assume you are as convinced as ever about the value of culture, which we're increasingly able to capture empirically, even quantitatively. More than that, we hope you feel empowered by something new and truly useful: a way to understand culture and to build an optimal one in your organization. As a leader, you want to leverage these natural functions toward a new way of doing things, one that emphasizes the critical need to build shared mental models. As we have explained before, the basic functions of any organization are vision, mission, capacity, and learning (VMCL). These are the foundational and critical mental models that must be shared in your organization via a cultural campaign. The North Star, the most important mental model of any organization's culture, is its vision. Second to this, in terms of importance and required focus, is building a shared mental model of the mission (the steps that, in repetition, achieve the vision). Capacity systems and learning are also sources of important mental models that form your culture. We like to say, in fact, that culture is your greatest capacity.

In other words, culture is the most critical resource in enabling your people to execute the mission to achieve the vision. Sharing mental models—which creates culture—is also the key mechanism for learning. Finally, it is critical that the most important tenets of your culture—V, M, C, and L—are aligned with one another. In other words, learning must build capacity to do mission to accomplish vision.

We hope it reminds you of the positive change you can have on both your individual employees and that which you seek to bring about in this world. Like many things we learn, or unlearn, success often relies on a unique combination of passion, practice (and more practice), and a bit of the reckless abandon that often disrupts industries and changes the world.

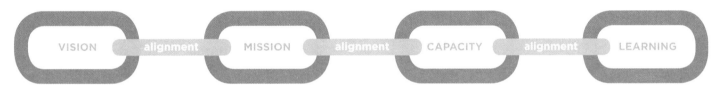

Figure 6.11: Four universal functions and three critical relationships

There are four important parts in VMCL that are obvious, but of equal power is the need to recognize and realize the incredible role the three relationships play in the success of implementing VMCL in your organization.

We hope that this book provides a new way of thinking about—and doing—your work across many levels of scale.

Armed with an understanding of the way you think, the way to build effective teams through thinking (and doing), and the transformational tools needed to lead your organization to become a truly adaptive learning organization, success is yours for the taking.

CHECK 20 **We create a culture of vision, mission, capacity, and learning**

Figure 6.12: Check for leading and building a VMCL culture

VMCL Checklist

Check #1: Our vision depicts a desired future state.

Check #2: Our vision is intrinsically motivating.

Check #3: Our vision is short and simple.

Check #4: We measure our vision.

Check #5: We ensure our vision lives in hearts and minds.

Check #6: Our mission is action(s) done repeatedly.

Check #7: Our mission brings about our vision.

Check #8: Our mission explains WHO does WHAT for WHOM.

Check #9: Our mission is clear, concise, and easily understood.

Check #10: We measure our mission.

Check #11: We ensure our mission lives in hearts and minds.

Check #12: We ensure that mission moments are sacrosanct.

Check #13: We build capacity in order to do our Mission.

Check #14 We build capacity through a system of systems.

Check #15 We map capacity to understand and better design systems.

Check #16 We use learning to expand our capacity.

Check #17: We harness the power of mental models.

Check #18: We train people to think in order to learn.

Check #19 We constantly evolve our mental models.

Check #20 We create a culture of vision, mission, capacity, and learning.

Do this with your executive team in a corporate offsite

Make sure your Vision meets these checks:

Check #1: Our vision depicts a desired future state.

Check #2: Our vision is intrinsically motivating.

Check #3: Our vision is short and simple.

Check #4: We measure our vision.

Make sure your Mission meets these checks:

Check #6: Our mission is action(s) done repeatedly.

Check #7: Our mission brings about our vision.

Check #8: Our mission explains WHO does WHAT for WHOM.

Check #9: Our mission is clear, concise, and easily understood.

Check #10: We measure our mission.

Do this in your culture everyday

Build a VMCL Culture

Check #5: We ensure our vision lives in hearts and minds.

Check #11: We ensure our mission lives in hearts and minds.

Check #12: We ensure that mission moments are sacrosanct.

Check #13: We build capacity in order to do our Mission.

Check #14 We build capacity through a system of systems.

Check #15 We map capacity to understand and better design systems.

Check #16 We use learning to expand our capacity.

Check #17: We harness the power of mental models.

Check #18: We train people to think in order to learn.

Check #19 We constantly evolve our mental models.

Check #20 We create a culture of vision, mission, capacity, and learning.

Figures

Figure 1.1: Smart global behavior is based on simple local rules. Cabrera

Figure 1.2: A superorganism's adaptive behavior is carried out by agents following simple rules. Cabrera

Figure 1.3: Complex adaptive system (CAS). Photo: Johan Sedig/iStock

Figure 1.4: 157,000+ fans set a world record for the largest human wave. Source Unknown

Figure 1.5: The basic features of a complex adaptive system. Cabrera

Figure 1.6: Reality bias. The grandfather of all biases. Cabrera

Figure 1.7: Contrasting mental models of process. Cabrera

Figure 1.8: Hierarchical org chart. Cabrera

Figure 1.9: Linear mental model versus nonlinear real world. Source In Dispute

Figure 1.10: Dynamic social network. Cabrera

Figure 1.11: Flow chart. Cabrera

Figure 1.12: Thinking drives Individual and Organizational Learning, which drives Capacity, which drives Mission, which brings about Vision. Cabrera

Figure 2.1: The visionless organization. kmlmtz66/Shutterstock

Figure 2.2: This vision is…sad. Cabrera

Figure 2.3: A sample of vision statements. Cabrera

Figure 2.4: How to tap intrinsic motivation: pop quiz. Cabrera

Figure 2.5: Original compressed map of MFP vision session. Cabrera

Figure 2.6: Original metamap of MFP vision session. Cabrera

Figure 2.7: Listing the measures for each element of your vision. Cabrera

Figure 2.8: The vision test. Cabrera

Figure 2.9: Where vision must reside. Frame photo: Gencho Petkov/Shutterstock, People photo : Pressmaster/Shutterstock

Figure 2.10: Early internal marketing for the vision. My Fitness Pal

Figure 2.11: Checks for a well-designed vision. Cabrera

Figure 3.1: Are we trying to make them bad? Randy Glasbergen

Figure 5.4: Learning is a feedback cycle. Cabrera

Figure 5.5: Learning: the feedback loop between reality and our mental models. Cabrera

Figure 5.6: Leaders of organizational learning lead from the pass. Cabrera

Figure 5.7: Mental models consolidate the meaning we make when we organize information using DSRP
(mental model = information + thinking). Cabrera

Figure 5.8: Alignment between learning and capacity completes the strong VMCL chain. Cabrera

Figure 5.9: Another way of saying thinking makes vision possible. Cabrera

Figure 5.10: Systems thinking/DSRP are metacognitive patterns that lie at the root of the many other types
of thinking we all want employees to possess. Cabrera

Figure 5.11: Which distinction do you want to make? Cabrera

Figure 5.12: Parts of a larger whole. Cabrera

Figure 5.13: Thinking through the parts of the Product Manager position we want to hire. Cabrera

Figure 5.14: A relationship exists between the Engineering team and the Customer (but what is it)? Cabrera

Figure 5.15: The Product Manager is the relationship between the Engineering team and the Customer. Cabrera

Figure 5.16: The Product Manager is a system and also a relationship between the Engineering team and the
Customer. Cabrera

Figure 5.17: A map showing the different mental models (perspectives) that different groups have about the same
software. Cabrera

Figure 5.18: OutThink, OutSync, OutDo, OutLast ideas. Cabrera

Figure 5.19: Plectica's cognitive architecture enhances thinking and clarity. Cabrera

Figure 5.20: Cognitive mapping of real-domains. Edelman

Figure 5.21: A concept map in the style of Joseph Novak. Novak

Figure 5.22: A meeting swarm occurs when a synchronous collaboration map facilitates discussion
(in person or virtual) in real time. Cabrera

Figure 5.23: Ideas and learning are collaborative and can be either synchronous or asynchronous. Cabrera

Figure 5.24: Map of a weekly meeting agenda. Cabrera

Figure 5.25: Canonical ideas can be inserted into maps in situ. Cabrera

Tables

Activities

Further Reading

Forward

Battilana, J., & Cascario, T. (2012). Change agents, networks, and institutions: A contingency theory of organizational change. *Academy of Management Journal, 55*(2), 381-398.

Conti, R. (2013). Frederick Winslow Taylor. In M. Witzel & M. Warner (Eds.), *The Oxford handbook of management theorists* (pp. 11-31). Oxford: Oxford University Press.

Fourteen principles of management. (n.d.). *Proven Models.* Retrieved from https://www.provenmodels.com/4/fourteen-principles-of-management/henri-fayol

Garvin, D. (2005). Building a learning organization. In French, W., Bell, C., & Jr., Zawacki, R. (Eds.). *Organization Development and Transformation: Managing Effective Change* (pp. 274-287). Boston: McGraw-Hill Irwin.

Getz, I. (2009). Liberating leadership: How the initiative-freeing radical organizational form has been successfully adopted. *California Management Review, 51*(4), 32-58.

Hazy, J., Goldstein, J., & Lichtenstein, B. (Eds.). (2007). *Complex systems leadership theory: New perspectives from complexity science on social and organizational effectiveness.* Mansfield, MA: ISCE Publishing.

Krames, J. (2003). *What the best CEOs know: 7 exceptional leaders and their lessons for transforming business.* New York: McGraw-Hill.

McGill, M. & Jr, Slocum, J. (1994). *The smarter organization: How to build a business that learns and adapts to marketplace needs.* Hoboken, NJ: John Wiley & Sons.

Perry, G.L. (2017, October 3). Human relations management theory basics. *Business.com.* Retrieved from https://www.business.com/articles/human-relations-management-theory-basics/

Popular Management Theories Decoded. (2017, June 27). *Business.com.* Retrieved from https://www.business.com/articles/popular-management-theories-decoded/

Schein, E. (2016). *Organizational culture and leadership* (5th ed.). Hoboken, NJ: John Wiley & Sons.

Chapter 1 Flock Not Clock

Dooley, K.J. (1997). A complex adaptive systems model of organizational change. *Nonlinear Dynamics, Psychology, and Life Sciences, 1*(1), 69-97.

Gell-Mann, M. (1994). Complex adaptive systems. In G. Cowan, D. Pines, and D. Meltzer (Eds.), *Complexity: Metaphors, models, and reality* (pp. 17-45). Boston, MA: Addison-Wesley.

Hazy, J., Goldstein, J., & Lichtenstein, B. (Eds.). (2007). *Complex systems leadership theory: New perspectives from complexity science on social and organizational effectiveness.* Mansfield, MA: ISCE Publishing.

Newman, M.E.J. (2003). The structure and function of complex networks. *Society for Industrial and Applied Mathematics, 45*(2), 167-256.

Rittel, H. W. J. & Webber, M. M. (1973). Dilemmas in a general theory of planning. *Policy Science, 4*(2), 155.

Stiehm, J. H., & Townsend, N. W. (2002). *The U.S. Army War College: Military education in a democracy.* Philadelphia, PA: Temple University Press.

Gell-Mann, M. (1988). The concept of the institute. In D. Pines (Ed.), *Emerging Synthesis in Science* (pp. 1–15). Reading, MA: Addison-Wesley.

Couzin, I.D., Krause, J., Franks, N.R. & Levin, S.A. (2005). Effective leadership and decision making in animal groups on the move. *Nature, 433*, 513-516.

Couzin, I.D. (2007). Collective minds. *Nature, 455*, 715.

Chapter 2 See Vision

Collins, J.C. & Porras, J.I. (1996, September-October). Building your company's vision. *Harvard Business Review.* Retrieved from https://hbr.org/1996/09/building-your-companys-vision

Geunpil Ryu. (2015.) The missing link of value congruence and its consequences: The mediating role of employees' acceptance of organizational vision. *Public Personnel Management, 44*(4), 473–495.

Howarth, M.D. & Rafferty, A.E. (2009). Transformational leadership and organizational change: The impact of vision content and delivery. *Academy of Management Annual Meeting Proceedings*, (1),1-6.

James, K. & Lahti, K. (2011). Organizational vision and system influences on employee inspiration and organizational performance. *Creativity and Innovation Management, 20*(2), 108-120.

Kenny, G. (2014, September 3). Your company's purpose is not its vision, mission, or values. *Harvard Business Review.* Retrieved from https://hbr.org/2014/09/your-companys-purpose-is-not-its-vision-mission-or-values

Khandelwal, K.A. & Mohendra, N. Espoused organizational values, vision, and corporate social responsibility: Does it matter to organizational members? *Vikalpa, 35*(3), 19-35.

Walesh, S.G. (2008). Vision: Pie-in-the-sky or organizational priority? *Leadership and Management in Engineering, 8*(1), 45-46.

Chapter 3 Do Mission

Holland, K. (2007, September 23). In mission statements, bizspeak and bromides. *The New York Times.* Retrieved from http://www.nytimes.com/2007/09/23/jobs/23mgmt.html

Kenny, G. (2014, September 3). Your company's purpose is not its vision, mission, or values. *Harvard Business Review.* Retrieved from https://hbr.org/2014/09/your-companys-purpose-is-not-its-vision-mission-or-values

Chapter 4 Align Capacity

Brown, T. (2008, June). Design thinking. *Harvard Business Review.* Retrieved from https://hbr.org/2008/06/design-thinking

Collier, K.W. (2011). *Agile analytics: A value-driven approach to business intelligence and data warehousing.* Boston, MA: Pearson Education.

Madden, L.T., Duchon, D., Madden, T.M. & Plowman, D.A. (2012). Emergent organizational capacity for compassion. *Academy of Management Review, 37*(4), 689-708.

Paynter, S. & Berner, M. (2014). Organizational capacity of nonprofit social service agencies. *Journal of Health and Human Services Administration, 37*(1), 111-45.

Taylor, F.W. (1911). *The principles of scientific management.* New York, New York: Harper & Brothers.

Chapter 5 Love Learning

Bersin, J. (2010, June 14). How to build a high-impact learning culture. *Bersin by Deloitte* [blog post]. Retrieved from http://blog.bersin.com/how-to-build-a-high-impact-learning-culture/

Bersin, J. (2012, January 18). 5 keys to building a learning organization. *Forbes.* Retrieved from https://www.forbes.com/sites/joshbersin/2012/01/18/5-keys-to-building-a-learning-organization

Chadwick, I.C. and Raver, J.L. (2015). Motivating organizations to learn: goal orientation and its influence on organizational learning. *Journal of Management, 41*(3), 957-986.

Chiva, R. and Habib, J. (2015). A framework for organizational learning: zero, adaptive and generative learning. *Journal of Management & Organization, 21*(3): 350-368.

Dalkir, K. (2011). *Knowledge management in theory and practice.* Oxford, UK: Elsevier.

Easterby-Smith, M. & Lyles, M. A. (2011). *Handbook of organizational learning and knowledge management.* Chichester, UK: Wiley.

Flores, L.G., Zheng, W., Rau, D. & Thomas, C.H. (2012). Organizational learning: Subprocesses identification, construct validation, and an empirical test of cultural antecedents. *Journal of Management, 38*(2), 640-667.

García-Morales, V.J, Jiménez-Barrionuevo, M.M & Gutiérrez-Gutiérrez, L. (2012). Transformational leadership influence on organizational performance through organizational learning. *Journal of Business Research, 65*, 1040-1050.

Garvin, D.A. (2005). Building a learning organization. In French, W., Bell, C.H. & Zawacki, R.A. (Eds.) *Organization development and transformation: Managing effective change* (pp. 274-287). Boston: McGraw-Hill Irwin.

Garvin, D.A., Edmondson, A.C. & Gino, F. (2008, March). Is yours a learning organization? *Harvard Business Review.* Retrieved from https://hbr.org/2008/03/is-yours-a-learning-organization

Joseph, D.L. & Newman, D.A. (2010). Emotional Intelligence: An Integrative Meta-Analysis and Cascading Model. *Journal of Applied Psychology, 95*(1), 54-78.

Lertpachin, C., Wingwon, B & Noithonglek, T. (2013). The effect of marketing focus, innovation and learning organization on the building of competitive advantages: empirical evidence from ISO 9000 certified companies. *Journal of Strategic Marketing, 21*(4), 323-331.

Nielson, B. (2015, March 11). Your learning culture is killing your company. *Your Training Edge.* Retrieved from http://www.yourtrainingedge.com/your-learning-culture-is-killing-your-company/

Novak, J. (1991). Clarify with concept maps. *The Science Teacher, 58*(7), 44.

Sarder, R. (2016). *Building an innovative learning organization: A framework to build a smarter workforce, adapt to change, and drive growth.* Hoboken, New Jersey: John Wiley & Sons, Inc.

Schulz, M. (2002). Organizational learning. In Joel A. C. Baum (Ed.), *Companion to organizations* (pp. 415-441). Oxford, UK: Blackwell Publishers.

Szostek, L. (2001, January 20). Create the learning organization. *Business Know-How.* Retrieved from http://www.businessknowhow.com/manage/learningorg.htm

Wang, Y. & Ellinger, A.D. (2011). Organizational learning: Perception of external environment and innovation performance. *International Journal of Manpower, 32*(5/6), 512-536.

Chapter 6 Leading a Culture Shift with VMCL

Adams, S. (2015, November 12). Corporate culture matters a lot, says new study. *Forbes.* Retrieved from https://www.forbes.com/sites/susanadams/2015/11/12/corporate-culture-matters-says-new-study

Alvesson, M., & Sveningsson, S. (2016). *Changing organizational culture: cultural change work in progress* (2nd ed.). New York, NY: Routledge.

Anderson, G. M., Anderson, M. J., & Lee, J. B. (2015, March/April). Defining corporate culture: Directors should understand the role of culture in business performance and whether culture and company strategy are aligned. *NACD online.* Retrieved from https://www.spencerstuart.com/-/media/pdf%20files/research%20and%20insight%20pdfs/defining-corpculture_30apr2015.pdf

Besner, G. (2015). Why company culture is more important than ever. *Entrepreneur.* Retrieved from https://www.entrepreneur.com/article/247522

Cancialosi, C. (2015, March 1). 4 questions that will define a lasting corporate culture. *Forbes.* Retrieved from https://www.forbes.com/sites/chriscancialosi/2015/03/02/4-questions-that-will-define-a-lasting-corporate-culture

Chatman, J. A., Caldwell, D.F., O'Reilly, C.A., & Doerr, B. (2014). Parsing organizational culture: How the norm for adaptability influences the relationship between culture consensus and financial performance in high-technology firms. *Journal of Organizational Behavior, 35*(6), 785-808.

Costanza, D., Blacksmith, N., Coats, M., Severt, J., & DeCostanza, A. (2016). The effect of adaptive organizational culture on long-term survival. *Journal of Business and Psychology, 31*(3).

Dosch, V., Goulet, W., & Finneman, T. (2015). *Wired differently: how to spark better results with a cooperative business model, servant leadership and shared values.* Oakville, Ontario: Milner & Associates.

Graham, J. R., Harvey, C. R., Popadak, J., & Rajgopal, S. (2015). Corporate culture: Evidence from the field. *Federal Reserve Bank of New York.* Retrieved from https://www.newyorkfed.org/medialibrary/media/research/conference/2015/econ_culture/Graham_Harvey_Popadak_Rajgopal.pdf

Heskett, J. (2012). *The culture cycle: how to shape the unseen force that transforms performance.* Upper Saddle River, NJ: FT Press.

Kelchner, L. (n.d.). Importance of a healthy corporate culture. *Chron.* Retrieved from http://smallbusiness.chron.com/importance-healthy-corporate-culture-20899.html

Kotter, J. (1996). *Leading change.* Boston, MA: Harvard Business School Press.

Krumholz, J. & Kreeger, S. (n.d.). Culture: your company's #1 asset. *Real HR Solutions.* Retrieved from http://realhrsolutions.com/culture-your-companys-1-asset/

O'Reilly, C.A., Caldwell, D.F., Chatman, J.A. & Doerr, B. (2014). The promise and problems of organizational culture. *Group & Organization Management, 39*(6), 614.

Ouchi, W.G. & Wilkins, A.L. (1985). Organizational culture. *Annual Review of Sociology, 111*(1), 457-483

Patrick, J. (2013, May 21). The real meaning of corporate culture. *The New York Times.* Retrieved from https://boss.blogs.nytimes.com/2013/05/21/the-real-meaning-of-corporate-culture

Schatsky, D. & Schwartz, J. (2015) Global human capital trends 2015 leading in the new world of work. *Deloitte University Press.* Retrieved from https://www2.deloitte.com/content/dam/Deloitte/at/Documents/human-capital/hc-trends-2015.pdf

Schein, E. H. (2010). *Organizational culture and leadership* (4th ed.). San Francisco: Jossey-Bass.

Silverthorne, S. (2011, September). The profit power of corporate culture. *Working knowledge: Business research for business leaders.* Cambridge, MA: Harvard Business School. Retrieved from http://hbswk.hbs.edu/item/the-profit-power-of-corporate-culture

Endnotes

CHAPTER ONE

[1] Couzin, I. D., Krause, J., James, R., Ruxton, G. D., & Franks, N. R. (2002). Collective memory and spatial sorting in animal groups. *Journal of Theoretical Biology, 218*(1), 1-11. doi:10.1006/yjtbi.3065

[2] Darwin, C. (1859). *On the origin of species by means of natural selection, or the preservation of favoured races in the struggle for life.* London: John Murray; Reprinted in Darwin, C. (1964). *On the origin of species: A facsimile of the first edition* (E. Mayr, Ed.). Cambridge, MA: Harvard University Press.

CHAPTER TWO

[1] Bregman, P. (2017, January 4).). Execution is a people problem, not a strategy problem. *Harvard Business Review.* Retrieved December 5, 2017, from https://hbr.org/2017/01/execution-is-a-people-problem-not-a-strategy-problem?utm_campaign=hbr&utm_source=facebook&utm_medium=social

[2] Carter, B. (2017, August 28). Employee engagement & loyalty statistics: The Ultimate Collection[Blog post]. *Access Perks.* Retrieved from http://blog.accessperks.com/employee-engagement-loyalty-statistics-the-ultimate-collection

[3] Vision attributes included future-orientation, brevity, clarity, ability to inspire, etc.

[4] Garcia, D. (2016, April 08). Under Armour CEO's big tip for starting a biz. Retrieved from https://www.cnbc.com/2016/04/08/under-armour-ceo-kevin-planks-big-tip-for-starting-a-biz.html

[5] Dermol, V. (2012). Relationship between mission statement and company performance. *Annals of the Alexandru Ioan Cuza University - Economics, 59*(1). doi:10.2478/v10316-012-0022-9

[6] Groscurth, C. (2014, March 6). Why your company must be mission-driven. *Gallup.* Retrieved from http://www.gallup.com/businessjournal/167633/why-company-mission-driven.aspx

[7] O'Boyle, E., & Mann, A. (2017, February 15). American workplace changing at a dizzying pace. *Gallup.* Retrieved from http://www.gallup.com/businessjournal/203957/american-workplace-changing-dizzying-pace.aspx

[8] Bowers, M. (2013, December 31). New survey: 58% of global employees don't know their company's vision. *Bollington Insurance.* Retrieved from https://www.bollington.com/mission-statement

[9] Groscurth, C. (2014, March 6). Why your company must be mission-driven. *Gallup.* Retrieved from http://www.gallup.com/businessjournal/167633/why-company-mission-driven.aspx

[10] Kouzes, J.M., & Posner, B. (2009, January 1). To lead, create a shared vision. *Harvard Business Review.* Retrieved from https://hbr.org/2009/01/to-lead-create-a-shared-vision

[11] The human era @ work: Findings from The Energy Project and Harvard Business Review. (2014) The Energy Project. Retrieved from https://uli.org/wp-content/uploads/ULI-Documents/The-Human-Era-at-Work.pdf

[12] Crabtree, S. (2013, October 8). Worldwide, 13% of employees are engaged at work. *Gallup.* Retrieved from http://www.gallup.com/poll/165269/worldwide-employees-engaged-work.aspx

[13] The human era @ work: Findings from The Energy Project and Harvard Business Review. (2014) The Energy Project. Retrieved from https://uli.org/wp-content/uploads/ULI-Documents/The-Human-Era-at-Work.pdf. The authors found that employees have "four predictable core needs at work: physically, to rest and renew; emotionally, to feel cared for and valued; mentally, to be empowered to set boundaries and focus in an absorbed way; and spiritually, to find a sense of meaning and purpose in their work." A total of 20,000 employees at all levels from multiple-sized organizations in more than 25 industries participated in the survey.

[14] The human era @ work: Findings from The Energy Project and Harvard Business Review. (2014) The Energy Project. Retrieved from https://uli.org/wp-content/uploads/ULI-Documents/The-Human-Era-at-Work.pdf

[15] Koloc, N. (2013, April 18). What job candidates really want: Meaningful work. *Harvard Business Review.* Retrieved from https://hbr.org/2013/04/what-job-candidates-really-wan

[16] This is highlighted when using a hierarchical org chart, which suggests alignment between principal and agent and therefore leads us to mistakenly expect compliance.

[17] Hechter, M., & Horne, C. (2009). *Theories of social order: A reader.* Stanford, CA: Stanford University Press.

[18] Nietzsche, F. W. (1998). *Twilight of the idols.* (D. Large, Trans.). Oxford: Oxford University Press. (Original work published in 1889)

[19] See, for example Follett, M. P. (2013). *Dynamic Administration.* Eastford, CT: Martino Publishing. (Original work published 1941); The Saylor Foundation. (n.d.). Historical and contemporary theories of management. Retrieved from https://learn.saylor.org/course/view.php?id=88&sectionid=6280

[20] Frankl, V. (2006). *Man's search for meaning.* Boston, MA: Beacon Press.

[21] Pink, D. (2011). *Drive: The surprising truth about what motivates us.* New York: Riverhead Books.

[22] Wagner, R., & Harter, J. (2007, December 13). The eighth element of great managing. *Gallup.* Retrieved from http://www.gallup.com/businessjournal/103084/eighth-element-great-managing.aspx

23 Amabile, T., & Kramer, S. (2012, December 19). To give your employees meaning, start with mission. *Harvard Business Review*. Retrieved from https://hbr.org/2012/12/to-give-your-employees-meaning.html

24 Collins, J. C. & Porras, J. I. (1991). Organizational vision and visionary organizations. *California Management Review, 50*, 31.

25 Kvidera, G., & Komen, M. (2003). Vision – mission, synonyms they are not! *Tips from the Top, 22* (4). Retrieved from http://kodyne.com/2012/10/30/vision-mission-synonyms-they-are-not/

26 Vision statement. (n.d.). In *Business Dictionary online*. Retrieved from http://www.businessdictionary.com/definition/vision-statement.html

27 Collins, J. C. & Porras, J. I. (1991). Organizational vision and visionary organizations. *California Management Review, 50*, 31.

28 Trammell, J. (2013, June 4). 5 Responsibilities of a CEO: Own the vision [Blog post]. Retrieved from http://theamericanceo.com/2013/06/04/the-5-responsibilities-of-a-ceo-own-the-vision/

29 See, for example Elliot, R. (2016, July 1). LinkedIn CEO shares his best business advice in letter to employees [Blog post]. *Conscious Culture Group*. Retrieved from https://www.consciousculturegroup.com/linkedin-vision-values-insights; PWC. (2015). 18th annual global CEO survey: A marketplace without boundaries? Retrieved from http://www.pwc.com/gx/en/ceosurvey/2015/assets/pwc-18th-annual-global-ceo-survey-jan-2015.pdf; University of MinnesotaLibraries Publishing. (2010). The roles of mission, vision, and values. *Principles of management*. Retrieved from https://open.lib.umn.edu/principlesmanagement/chapter/4-3-the-roles-of-missionvision-and-

30 Kasowski, B., & Filion, L.J. (2010). A Study of the 2005 Fortune 500 Vision Statements. (Rogers – J.A.-Bombardier Chair of Entrepreneurship Working Paper Series, No. 2010-04) Retrieved from http://expertise.hec.ca/chaire_entrepreneuriat/wp-content/uploads/2010-04-cahier-vision-fortune-500.pdf

31 Mission, vision, and values. (n.d.). *The Coca-Cola Company*. Retrieved from http://www.cocacolacompany.com/our-company/mission-vision-values

32 Zacks Equity Research. (2010, June 9). Caterpillar updates vision 2020. Retrieved from https://www.zacks.com/stock/news/35363/caterpillar-updates-vision-2020

33 The group's strategy. (2011). *Volkswagen Poznan*. Retrieved from http://www.volkswagen-poznan.pl/en/groups-strategy

34 Fernandes, P. (2017, April 10). What is a vision statement? *Business News Daily*. Retrieved from http://www.businessnewsdaily.com/3882-vision-statement.html

35 Marr, B. (2013). What the heck is wrong with... mission and vision statements? Retrieved from https://www.linkedin.com/pulse/20130626044531-64875646-what-the-hell-is-wrong-with-mission-andvision-statements

36 Collins, J. C. & Porras, J. I. (1991). Organizational vision and visionary organizations. *California Management Review, 50*, 31.

37 Fernandes, P. (2017, April 10). What is a vision statement? *Business News Daily*. Retrieved from http://www.businessnewsdaily.com/3882-vision-statement.html

38 Collins, J. C. & Porras, J. I. (1991). Organizational vision and visionary organizations. *California Management Review, 50*, 31.

39 As Collins and Porras (1991) explain: "However, even though purpose is always present—in the woodwork—and many successful companies have not explicitly articulated it, we firmly believe that any company will benefit tremendously by the exercise of identifying and writing down a concise, complete statement of purpose."

40 Vision [Def. 1, 2, & 3]. (n.d.). *In Dictionary.com*. Retrieved from http://www.dictionary.com/browse/vision

41 The majority of corporate visions do not have an expiration date on them, though as we noted, some organizations and consultants recommend five- or 10-year visions. We recommend that your vision change less often than the particulars of your mission, capacity, or learning, but as often as is necessary based on feedback from the environment. That's what an adaptive organization does—it changes when necessary, not on the basis of simplistic heuristics of when it should change.

42 Romero, J. L. (n.d.). Sample vision statements. [Blog post]. *Skills2Lead*. Retrieved from http://www.skills2lead.com/sample-vision-statements.html

43 Amortegui, J. (2014, June 26). Why finding meaning at work is more important than feeling happy. *Fast Company*. Retrieved from https://www.fastcompany.com/3032126/how-to-find-meaning-during-your-pursuit-of-happiness-at-work

44 Folkman, J. (2014, April 22). 8 ways to ensure your vision is valued. *Forbes*. Retrieved from https://www.forbes.com/sites/joefolkman/2014/04/22/8-ways-to-ensure-your-vision-is-valued

45 Corporate governance principles. (2017, August 10) *Dean Foods*. Retrieved from http://www.deanfoods.com/our-company/investor-relations/corporate-governance/principles.aspx as cited in: Amabile, T., & Kramer, S. (2012, December 19). To give your employees meaning, start with mission. *Harvard Business Review*. Retrieved from https://hbr.org/2012/12/to-give-your-employeesmeaning.html Honda's 1970 vision comes from: Romero, J. L. (n.d.). Sample vision statements. [Blog post]. *Skills2Lead*. Retrieved from http://www.skills2lead.com/sample-vision-statements.html

46 Cabrera, D. (2013, December). Personal conversation with MFP executive team.

47 Kotter, J. (2013, October 14). Your company vision: if it's complicated, it shouldn't be. *Forbes*. Retrieved from https://www.forbes.com/sites/johnkotter/2013/10/14/the-reason-most-company-vision-statements-arent-effective

48 Our vision. (n.d.). Nestlé. Retrieved December 6, 2017, from http://www.nestle.com/randd/ourvision

49 Pape, L. (n.d.). End veteran homelessness. *Performance*. Retrieved from https://www.performance.gov/content/end-veteran-homelessness

[50] The mission statement: Do employees get your company? (n.d.). *Monster.com*. Retrieved from https://hiring.monster.com/hr/hr-best-practices/workforce-management/employee-performance-management/mission-statement.aspx. Adapted from Catlette, B., & Hadden, R. (2012). *Contented cows still give better milk: the plain truth about employee engagement and your bottom line*. Hoboken, NJ: John Wiley & Sons.

[51] Office Depot's vision provides a good example of the particular meaning that organizational members attach to the words of the vision statement. Office Depot's vision (Delivering Winning Solutions that Inspire Worklife) includes several sentences to explain every word of their vision. See Romero, J. L. (n.d.). Sample vision statements. [Blog post]. *Skills2Lead*. Retrieved from http://www.skills2lead.com/sample-vision-statements.html

[52] Christensen, C. [claychristensen]. (2015, February 20). Purpose must be deliberately conceived and chosen, and then pursued [Twitter post]. Retrieved from https://twitter.com/leadinnovation/status/568810114037239808

[53] If you don't get this reference, please watch the 90-second "I love this company" video on YouTube: https://www.youtube.com/watch?v=f__n8084YAE

[54] Collins, J. C. & Porras, J. I. (1991). Organizational vision and visionary organizations. *California Management Review, 50*, 31.

[55] McAveeney, C. (2013) How do you define startup culture? *Wired*. Retrieved from https://www.wired.com/insights/2013/09/how-do-you-define-startup-culture/

CHAPTER THREE

[1] Adams, S. (1996). *The Dilbert principle: A cubicle's-eye view of bosses, meetings, management fads & other workplace afflictions*. New York: HarperCollins.

[2] Zetlin, M. (2013, November 15). The 9 worst mission statements of all time. *Inc.* Retrieved from http://www.inc.com/minda-zetlin/9-worst-mission-statements-all-time.html; Blakeman, C. (2015, May 25).Why most mission statements suck so bad. Inc. Retrieved from http://www.inc.com/chuck-blakeman/why-most-mission-statements-suck-so-bad.html

[3] Kohli, S. (2014, July 17). When Weird Al Yankovic sings about business jargon, he's mocking these companies. *Quartz*. Retrieved from https://qz.com/236031/when-weird-al-yankovic-mockscsny-flavored-business-jargon-hes-singing-about-these-companies/. Watch the YouTube video: https://youtu.be/GyV_UG60dD4 (spoiler: it's a parody of a Crosby, Stills, Nash, & Young song).

[4] Federman, B. (2014, December 1). Why I hate mission statements—but love missions. *Association for Talent Development*. Retrieved from https://www.td.org/insights/why-i-hate-mission-statementsbut-love-missions

[5] Shults, J. F. (2012, September 28). 5 things I hate about department mission statements. *Police One*. Retrieved from https://www.policeone.com/chiefs-sheriffs/articles/5994593-5-things-I-hate-aboutdepartment-mission-statements/

[6] Knight, S. (2015). *Life-changing magic of not giving a f*ck: How to stop spending time you don't have with people you don't like doing things you don't want to do.* London: Quercus.

[7] Glasbergen, R. (n.d.). Mission statements. [Cartoon]. Retrieved from http://www.glasbergen.com/business-computer-cartoons/mission-statements/

[8] Mission Statements online. (2016, September 30). Create a mission statement. Retrieved from https://www.missionstatements.com/mission-statement-accelerator.html

[9] Drucker, P. (1973). *Management: Tasks, responsibilities, practices.* New York: Harper & Row.

[10] Tribby, M. (2016, September 6). Is your business confused? [Blog post]. *The Huffington Post*. Retrieved from http://www.huffingtonpost.com/maryellen-tribby/is-your-business-confused_b_11879092.html

[11] Abrahams, J. (2001). *The mission statement book: 302 corporate mission statements from America's top companies.* Berkeley, CA: Ten Speed Press, as cited in Jenkins, M. (2005, October). Powerplay. *BlackEnterprise.com*.

[12] Fishburne, T. (2011, January 30). *Mission statement.* [Cartoon]. *Marketoonist.* Retrieved from https://marketoonist.com/2011/01/mission-statement.html

[13] See, for example Pearce II, J. A., & David, F. (1987). Corporate mission statements: the bottom line. *Academy of Management Executive, 1*(2), 109-115. doi:10.5465/AME.1987.4275821; Verma, H. V. (2009). Mission statements: a study of intent and influence. *Journal of Services Research, 9*(2), 153-72.

[14] Bart, C. K., & Baetz, M. C. (1998). The relationship between mission statements and firm performance: an exploratory study. *Journal of Management Studies, 35*(6), 825.

[15] Hoagland-Smith, L. (n.d.). Why confusion between vision and mission statements hurts sales growth and sales managers [Blog post]. *Evan Carmichael*. Retrieved from http://www.evancarmichael.com/library/leanne-hoagland-smith/Why-Confusion-Between-Vision-and-Mission-Statements-Hurts-Sales-Growth-and-Sales-Managers.htmlSales-Growth-and-Sales-Managers.html

[16] Federman, B. (2014, December 1). Why I hate mission statements—but love missions. *Association for Talent Development*. Retrieved from https://www.td.org/insights/why-i-hate-mission-statementsbut-love-missions

[17] Emery, M. (1996). Mission control. *Training and Development, 50* (7), 51–53.

[18] Emery, M. (1996). Mission control. *Training and Development, 50* (7), 51–53.

[19] Gallup releases new findings on the state of the American workplace. *Gallup*. (2013, June 11). Retrieved from http://www.gallup.com/opinion/gallup/170570/gallup-releases-new-findings-state-americanworkplace.aspx

[20] For a brief summary, see Desmidt, S., & Prinzie, A. A. (August 2009). The effectiveness of mission statements: an explorative analysis from a communication perspective. *Academy of Management AnnualMeeting Proceedings, 1-6.* doi:10.5465/AMBPP.2009.44257947

[21] Bart, C. K., Bontis, N., & Taggar, S. (2001). A model of the impact of mission statements on firm performance. *Management Decision, 39*(1), 19–35. Retrieved from http://www.emeraldinsight.com/doi/abs/10.1108/EUM0000000005404

[22] Weller, C. (2016, August 24). A Harvard psychologist reveals the biggest reason people don't achieve their goals. *Business Insider.* Retrieved from http://www.businessinsider.com/biggest-goal-setting-mistake-amy-cuddy-2016-8

[23] Arthur, L. (n.d.). What are the elements of a strong corporate culture? *Chron.* Retrieved from http://smallbusiness.chron.com/elements-strong-corporate-culture-15674.html

[24] Roach, T. J. (2009). A proper mission statement helps a company achieve its mission. *Rock Products, 112*(4), 6.

[25] Durant, W. (1961). *The story of philosophy: the lives and opinions of the greater philosophers.* New York: Pocket Books.

[26] Gardiner, L. (n.d.). From synchilla to school support: Outdoor clothing manufacturer Patagonia
recognized for corporate responsibility. Santa Clara University. Retrieved from https://legacy.scu.edu/ethics/publications/iie/v8n1/synchilla.html

[27] This component of Patagonia's mission would appear to pose the greatest measurement challenge, perhaps necessitating an internal survey on customer inspiration.

[28] Patagonia. (n.d.). Patagonia's mission statement. Retrieved from http://www.patagonia.com/company-info.html

[29] Our strategy. (n.d.). *Carillion.* Retrieved from http://www.carillion.ca/about-us/our-strategy.aspx

[30] Schwartz, G. (2017, January 26). 'Do your job' is why the Patriots can win with anybody. *SBNation.* Retrieved from https://www.sbnation.com/2017/1/26/14390366/patriots-do-your-job-mantra-super-bowl-2017-what-it-means

[31] We are of course not against missions being "inspirational" or "distinguishing oneself from close competitors." (Indeed, we have found that organizations that follow our rules for crafting their missions often end up with inspirational ones.) If those two benefits unwittingly result from a well-crafted mission, that's great fortune. But they do not represent the central utility of the mission. Similarly, "Do Your Job" widely inspires Patriot Nation, but we highly doubt that was the goal. Winning the Super Bowl (the vision) is all the inspiration the Patriots need.

[32] Porras, J. I., & Collins, J. C. (1994). *Built to last: successful habits of visionary companies.* New York: HarperCollins.

[33] McCurdy, E. (1906). *Leonardo Da Vinci's note-books: Arranged and rendered into English with introductions.* New York: Charles Scribner's Sons.

[34] Toffler, A. (1970). *Future shock.* New York: Bantam Books.

[35] Welch, J. (2015, May 5). Three ways to take your company's pulse [Blog post]. *Jack Welch Management Institute.* Retrieved from http://winning.jwmi.com/three-ways-take-company-pulse/

[36] The sharing of these visions should not be interpreted as endorsement, political commentary, or anything else that might piss people or rabbits off.

[37] Petro, G. (2016, August 25). Amazon vs. Walmart: clash of the titans. *Forbes.* Retrieved from https://www.forbes.com/sites/gregpetro/2016/08/25/amazon-vs-walmart-clash-of-the-titans

[38] McMillon, D. (2017, January 6). 3 predictions for the future of retail – from the CEO of Walmart. *World Economic Forum.* Retrieved from https://www.weforum.org/agenda/2017/01/3-predictions-forthe-future-of-retail-from-the-ceo-of-walmart/. However, an outside source provides the following mission and vision for Walmart — Vision: "To be the best retailer in the hearts and minds of consumers and employees." Mission: "Saving people money so they can live better." Cited from Ferguson, E. (2017, March 25). Walmart's vision, mission, generic & intensive strategies. *Panmore Institute.* Retrieved from http://panmore.com/walmart-vision-mission-statement-intensive-generic-strategies

[39] Verma, H. V. (2009). Mission statements: A study of intent and influence. *Journal of Services Research, 9*(2), 154.

[40] Keep an open mind about what we mean by customer. When we say "who or what" the mission is being done for, this incorporates a wide range of things. While for most companies it's their customer base, it could also be a national park, a country, Earth, an art collection, an animal species, a principle or ideal, etc. The blurring of private and public in all sectors leads to organizational missions performed for a mix of "whos and whats."

[41] Amortegui, J. (2014, March 27). 5 reasons you need to instill values in your organization. *Fast Company.* Retrieved from http://www.fastcompany.com/3028201/leadership-now/5-reasons you-need-to-instill-values-in-your-organization

[42] Emery, M. (1996). Mission control. *Training and Development, 50* (7), 51–53.

[43] Romero, J. L. (n.d.). Sample vision statements. [Blog post]. *Skills2Lead.* Retrieved from http://www.skills2lead.com/sample-vision-statements.html

[44] Bumiller, E. (2010, April 26). We have met the enemy and he is PowerPoint. *The New York Times.* Retrieved from http://www.nytimes.com/2010/04/27/world/27powerpoint.html?_r=0

[45] Hogge, T. (2014, November 19). What I learned about leadership from a 4-star general. *Business Insider.* Retrieved from http://www.businessinsider.com/leadership-lessons-from-a-4-star-general-2014-11

46 Mission statement. (n.d.). *Business Resource Software, Inc.* Retrieved from http://businessplans.org/guide/mission/

47 Our company. (n.d.). *Asana.* Retrieved from https://asana.com/company

48 Mission, vision, and values. (n.d.). *The Coca-Cola Company.* Retrieved from http://www.cocacolacompany.com/our-company/mission-vision-values

49 Cameron, W.B. (1963). *Informal sociology: a casual introduction to sociological thinking.* New York: Random House.

50 Knufken, D. (2011, March 22). 100 funny business quotes. *Business Pundit.* Retrieved from http://www. businesspundit.com/100-funny-business-quotes/

51 Funny inspirational quotes: hilarious but motivational quotations [Blog post]. (2015, September 11) *Ignited Quotes.* Retrieved from http://www.ignitedquotes.com/funny-inspirational-quotes/

52 McManus, K. (2000). Your mission (must you accept it?). *IIE Solutions, 32*(1), 20.

53 Groscurth, C. (2014, March 6). Why your company must be mission-driven. *Business Journal.* Retrieved from http://www.gallup.com/businessjournal/167633/why-company-mission-driven. aspx

CHAPTER FOUR

1 Capacity is about a state of being, and learning is a reflective process of thinking about something, which is why we sometimes refer to Vision, Mission, Capacity, and Learning by the mnemonic, "See, Do, Be, Re."

2 Hamel, G., & Zanini, M. (2016, September 5). Excess management is costing the U.S. $3 trillion per year. *Harvard Business Review.* Retrieved from https://hbr.org/2016/09/excess-management-is-costingthe-us-3-trillion-per-year

3 Hamel, G., & Zanini, M. (2016, September 5). Excess management is costing the U.S. $3 trillion per year. *Harvard Business Review.* Retrieved from https://hbr.org/2016/09/excess-management-is-costingthe-us-3-trillion-per-year

4 Hamel, G., & Zanini, M. (2016, September 5). Excess management is costing the U.S. $3 trillion per year. *Harvard Business Review.* Retrieved from https://hbr.org/2016/09/excess-management-is-costingthe-us-3-trillion-per-year

5 Himmelstein, D.H., Jun, M., Busse, R., Chevre, K., Geissler, A., Jeurissen, P., et al. (2014). A comparison of hospital administrative costs in eight nations: US costs exceed all others by far. Health Affairs, 33(9). doi.org/10.1377/hlthaff.2013.1327

6 Dig deeper. organic pioneer: Alice Waters. (2013, August 29)R. odale Institute. Retrieved from https://rodaleinstitute.org/organic-pioneer-alice-waters/

7 Leavenworth, S. (2009, May 28). The chef apprentice: after 37 years, Alice Waters still searches for a slow food life. *Sacramento Bee.* Retrieved from https://web.archive.org/web/20111008005733/http://www.sacbee.com/static/weblogs/the_chef_apprentice/2009/05/after-37-years-alice-waters-st.html/022626.html

8 Dig deeper. organic pioneer: Alice Waters. (2013, August 29)R. odale Institute. Retrieved from https://rodaleinstitute.org/organic-pioneer-alice-waters/

9 Alice Waters: 40 years of sustainable food. (2011, August 22). *NPR Fresh Air.* Retrieved from https://www.npr.org/2011/08/22/139707078/alice-waters-40-years-of-sustainable-food

10 The Sysco Story. (n.d.) *Sysco.* Retrieved from http://www.sysco.com/about-sysco.html

11 About Chez Panisse. (n.d.). *Chez Panisse.* Retrieved from http://www.chezpanisse.com/about/chezpanisse/

12 About Chez Panisse. (n.d.). *Chez Panisse.* Retrieved from http://www.chezpanisse.com/about/chezpanisse/

13 Leavenworth, S. (2009, May 28). The chef apprentice: after 37 years, Alice Waters still searches for a slow food life. *Sacramento Bee.* Retrieved from https://web.archive.org/web/20111008005733/http://www.sacbee.com/static/weblogs/the_chef_apprentice/2009/05/after-37-years-alice-waters-st.html/022626.html

14 Leavenworth, S. (2009, May 28). The chef apprentice: after 37 years, Alice Waters still searches for a slow food life. *Sacramento Bee.* Retrieved from https://web.archive.org/web/20111008005733/http://www.sacbee.com/static/weblogs/the_chef_apprentice/2009/05/after-37-years-alice-waters-st.html/022626.html

15 Beer, S (2002). What is cybernetics? *Kybernetes, 31*(2): 209–219. doi:10.1108/03684920210417283.

16 Another systems-thinking maxim is that "system structure determines behavior." A very physical example is organizing offices around an atrium to encourage interaction and collaboration. The idea is that if your system isn't building the kind of capacity you need, pay attention to its structure.

17 Blett, T., Geiser, L., & Porter, E. (2003). Air pollution-related lichen monitoring in national parks, forests, and refuges: guidelines for studies intended for regulatory and management purposes. *U.S. Departmentof the Interior & U.S. Department of Agriculture.* Retrieved from http://www.nature.nps.gov/air/pubs/pdf/Lichen_Studies.pdf

18 Lichens as bioindicators. (1997). *Technical Education Research Centers.* Retrieved from https://staff.concord.org/~btinker/gaiamatters/investigations/lichens/lichens.html

19 System [Def. 1]. (n.d.). *Dictionary.com.* Retrieved from http://www.dictionary.com/browse/system

20 Pugh, D., & Hickson D. (2016.) *Great writers on organizations: the third omnibus edition.* Boca Raton, FL: CRC Press.

21 See, for example Department. (n.d.) *Online Etymology Dictionary.* Retrieved from https://www.etymonline.com/word/department; and Depart. (n.d.). Wiktionary. Retrieved fromhttps://en.wiktionary.org/wiki/depart

22 Carbary, J. (2016, June 27). The secret to setting goals for your sales team. Retrieved from https://www.linkedin.com/pulse/secret-setting-goals-your-sales-team-james-carbary

23 Lencioni, P. M. (2002). Make your values mean something. *Harvard Business Review, July.* Retrieved from https://hbr.org/2002/07/make-your-values-mean-something. The article credits Built to Last, arguing that "The book made the case that many of the best companies adhered to a set of principles called core values, provoking managers to stampede to off-site meetings in order to conjure up some core values of their own."

24 Lencioni, P. M. (2002). Make your values mean something. *Harvard Business Review, July.* Retrieved from https://hbr.org/2002/07/make-your-values-mean-something.

25 Wendy. (2013, March 12). Company core values: why to have them and how to define them [Blog post]. *7 Geese.* Retrieved from https://7geese.com/benefits-of-having-core-values-and-how-to-set-them-in-your-organization/

26 Ruiz, M. (1997). *The four agreements: A practical guide to personal freedom.* San Rafael, CA. : Amber-Allen Publishing.

27 REI has made Fortune's "100 Best Companies to Work For" annually since rankings began in 1998. They write: "At REI, we inspire, educate and outfit for a lifetime of outdoor adventure and stewardship." About REI. (n.d.) *REI.* Retrieved from https://www.rei.com/about-rei.html

28 Patel, S. (2015, August 6). 10 examples of companies with fantastic cultures. *Entrepreneur.com.* Retrieved from https://www.entrepreneur.com/article/249174

29 Fisher, M. (2010, April 28). Why the military declared war on Powerpoint. *The Atlantic.* Retrieved from https://www.theatlantic.com/politics/archive/2010/04/why-the-military-declared-war-on-powerpoint/345802/

30 Neill, C. (2012, November 30). Amazon staff meetings: "no powerpoint" [Blog post]. *Conor Neill.* Retrieved from https://conorneill.com/2012/11/30/amazon-staff-meetings-no-powerpoint

31 Amazon.com, Inc. (1998, April 24). Exhibit 99.1. Retrieved from SEC EDGAR website https://www.sec.gov/Archives/edgar/data/1018724/000119312518121161/d456916dex991.htm

32 Bhuiyan, J. (2017, February 21). How Uber got into this human resources mess. *Recode.* Retrieved from https://www.recode.net/2017/2/21/14673658/uber-travis-kalanick-susan-fowler-diversity-sexual-harassment

CHAPTER FIVE

1 Marieb, E. N., & Hoehn, K. (2007). *Human anatomy & physiology* (7th ed.). San Francisco: Pearson Benjamin Cummings.

2 Or it can provide cognitive structures that are maladaptive. Edward Tufte's work on the [maladaptive] cognitive style of PowerPoint is a brilliant piece of research on how the underlying structure of PowerPoint actually causes us to decrease the effectiveness of our thinking and leads to increased miscommunications. Tufte, E. R. (2003). *The cognitive style of PowerPoint.* Cheshire, CT:Graphics Press.

3 Fleming, S. M. (2014). Metacognition is the forgotten secret to success. *Scientific American Mind, 25*(5), 30–37. doi.org/10.1038/scientificamericanmind0914-30.

4 Dying to be Barbie: eating disorders in pursuit of the impossible. (n.d.) *Rehabs online.* Retrieved from https://www.rehabs.com/explore/dying-to-be-barbie

5 Norton, K. I., Olds, T. S., Olive, S., & Dank S. (1996). Ken and Barbie at life size. *Sex Roles, 34,* 287–294. doi.org/10.1007/BF01544300

6 Dittmar, H., Halliwell, E., & Ive, S. (2006). Does Barbie make girls want to be thin? The effect of experimental exposure to images of dolls on the body image of 5- to 8-year-old girls. *Developmental Psychology, 42*(2), 283–292. doi:10.1037/0012-1649.42.2.283

7 Our mission. (n.d.). *Lammily, LLC.* Retrieved from https://lammily.com/about/our-mission/

8 Pillay, D., Naicker, I., & Pithouse-Morgan, K. (2016). *Academic autoethnographies: inside teaching in higher education.* Rotterdam, The Netherlands:SensePublishers.

9 Have you gone noseblind? (n.d.) *Procter & Gamble.* Retrieved from http://febreze.com/en-us/learn/have-you-gone-noseblind

10 Cohan, P. (2012). Jurassic Park: how P&G brought Febreze back to life. *Forbes.* Retrieved from https://www.forbes.com/sites/petercohan/2012/02/19/jurassic-park-how-pg-broughtfebreze-back-to-life

11 Cohan, P. (2012). Jurassic Park: how P&G brought Febreze back to life. *Forbes.* Retrieved from https://www.forbes.com/sites/petercohan/2012/02/19/jurassic-park-how-pg-broughtfebreze-back-to-life

12 Cohan, P. (2012). Jurassic Park: how P&G brought Febreze back to life. *Forbes.* Retrieved from https://www.forbes.com/sites/petercohan/2012/02/19/jurassic-park-how-pg-broughtfebreze-back-to-life

13 Case Study: Old Spice Response Campaign. (n.d.). *D&AD.* Retrieved from https://www.dandad.org/en/d-ad-old-spice-case-study-insights/

14 Gold Standards. (n.d.). *The Ritz-Carlton.* Retrieved from http://www.ritzcarlton.com/en/about/gold-standards

[15] Harris, I. (2015, April 27). 'WOW' stories: How Ritz-Carlton brings its values to life. *Gatehouse*. Retrieved from http://www.gatehouse.co.uk/wow-stories-how-ritz-carlton-brings-its-values-to-life/

[16] Guest story: A new family [Blog post]. (2015, December 23). *The Ritz-Carlton Leadership Institute*. Retrieved from http://ritzcarltonleadershipcenter.com/2015/12/guest-story-a-new-family/

[17] Cross, J. (n.d.). Where did the 80% come from? [Blog post]. *Informal Learning Blog*. Retrieved from http://www.informl.com/where-did-the-80-come-from

[18] Gino, F. (2015, September 15). The unexpected influence of stories told at work. *Harvard Business Review*. Retrieved from https://hbr.org/2015/09/the-unexpected-influence-of-stories-told-at-work

[19] Tax, S. S., & Brown, S. W. (1998). Recovering and learning from service failure. *Sloan Management Review, 40*(1). Retrieved from sloanreview.mit.edu/article/recovering-and-learning-from-service-failure/

[20] Hoffman, J. (2014, May 8). Secrets of the Ritz-Carlton's 'legendary' customer service. *PSA Financial Services Inc.* Retrieved from https://www.psafinancial.com/2018/02/employee-engagement-ritz-carltons-secret-world-class-service-customer-loyalty/

[21] Barsh, J., Capozzi, M. M., & Davidson, J. (2008). Leadership and innovation. *McKinsey Quarterly*. Retrieved from http://www.mckinsey.com/business-functions/strategy-and-corporate-finance/our-insights/leadership-and-innovation

[22] Senge, P. M. (1990). *The fifth discipline: the art and practice of the learning organization*. New York: Doubleday.

[23] The New Science of Leadership: An Interview with Margaret Wheatley [Interview by S. London]. (1997, January). Retrieved December 11, 2017, from http://www.scottlondon.com/interviews/wheatley.html

[24] Wonacott, M. E. (2000). The learning organization: theory and practice (Vol. 12, Myths and Realities, pp. 3-4, Publication No. 071). Columbus, OH: ERIC Clearinghouse on Adult, Career, and Vocational Education. (ERIC Document Reproduction Service No. ED448293).

[25] Otala, M. (1995). The learning organization: theory into practice (Vol. 9, Industry and Higher Education, pp. 157-164, Publication No. 3). (ERIC Document Reproduction Service No. EJ505970).

[26] Garratt, B. (1999). The learning organisation 15 years on: some personal reflections. (Vol. 6, The Learning Organization, pp. 202-207, Publication No. 5). (ERIC Document Reproduction Service No. EJ612474) https://doi.org/10.1108/09696479910299802.

[27] Garvin, D. A. (1993, July-August). Building a learning organization. *Harvard Business Review*. Retrieved from https://hbr.org/1993/07/building-a-learning-organization.

[28] Garvin, D. A. (1993, July-August). Building a learning organization. *Harvard Business Review*. Retrieved from https://hbr.org/1993/07/building-a-learning-organization.

[29] Ramos-Aquino, M. (2015, June 19). The future of learning. *The Manila Times*. Retrieved from http://www.manilatimes.net/the-future-of-learning/193360/

[30] Grossman, R. J. (2015, May 1). How to create a learning culture. *Society for Human Resource Management*. Retrieved from https://www.shrm.org/hr-today/news/hr-magazine/pages/0515-learning-culture.aspx

[31] This book has a sister book on DSRP called Systems Thinking Made Simple. And, DSRP has been developed into software and numerous other tools that are freely available. A thorough dive into the benefits of DSRP and how it works can be better found in these resources. However, for the uninitiated, we will provide a short section on DSRP here.

[32] Stephenson, K. (2009). Neither hierarchy nor network: an argument for heterarchy. *People + Strategy, 32*(1).

[33] Wagner, R., & Harter, J. (2008, April 10). The twelfth element of great managing. *Gallup*. Retrieved from http://www.gallup.com/businessjournal/105838/Twelfth-Element-Great-Managing.aspx

[34] Wagner, R., & Harter, J. (2008, April 10). The twelfth element of great managing. *Gallup*. Retrieved from http://www.gallup.com/businessjournal/105838/Twelfth-Element-Great-Managing.aspx

[35] Robison, J. (2007, July 12). The business value of learning. *Gallup*. Retrieved from http://news.gallup.com/businessjournal/28069/business-value-learning.aspx

[36] Robison, J. (2007, July 12). The business value of learning. *Gallup*. Retrieved from http://news.gallup.com/businessjournal/28069/business-value-learning.aspx

[37] Gell-Mann, M. (1995). Let's call it plectics. *Complexity, 1*(5), 3.

[38] Montessori, M. (1949). *The absorbent mind*. New York: Holt Publishing.

[39] Edelman, S. (2018). Computing the mind: Lecture 7.2, Psych/Cogst/Info2140/6140. Cornell University, Ithaca, NY.

[40] Tolman, E.C. (1948). Cognitive maps in rats and men. *Psychological Review, 55*, 189-208.

[41] Eden, C. (1992). On the nature of cognitive maps. *Journal of Management Studies, 29*(3), 261-265.

[42] Eden, C., Jones, S., & Sims, D. (1979). *Thinking in organizations*. London: Macmillan.

[43] Novak, J.D., & Cañas, A.J. (2006). The origins of the concept mapping tool and the continuing evolution of the tool. *Information Visualization, 5*, 175-184.

44 Neill, C. (2012, November 30). Amazon staff meetings: "no powerpoint" [Blog post]. *Conor Neill.* Retrieved from https://conorneill.com/2012/11/30/amazon-staff-meetings-no-powerpoint

45 Tufte, E. R. (2003). *The cognitive style of PowerPoint.* Cheshire, CT:Graphics Press.

46 Beni G., & Wang J. (1993). Swarm Intelligence in Cellular Robotic Systems.In: Dario P., Sandini G., Aebischer P. (Eds.) Robots and Biological Systems: Towards a New Bionics? NATO ASI Series (Series F: Computer and Systems Sciences), vol 102. Berlin: Springer-Verlag.

47 Gell-Mann, M. (1995). *The quark and the jaguar: Adventures in the simple and the complex.* New York, New York: W.H. Freeman and Co.

CHAPTER SIX

1 Chesky, B. (2014, April 20). Don't fuck up the culture [Blog post]. *Medium.* Retrieved from https://medium.com/@bchesky/dont-fuck-up-the-culture-597cde9ee9d4

2 Cancialosi, C. (2015, June 22). 5 myths about organizational culture every CEO should know. *Forbes.* Retrieved from https://www.forbes.com/sites/chriscancialosi/2015/06/22/5-mythsabout-organizational-culture-every-ceo-should-know

3 Gerstner, L.V., Jr. (2002). *Who says elephants can't dance: Inside IBM's historic turnaround.* New York, NY: HarperCollins Publishers, Inc.

4 Durkheim's sociological understanding of culture has been described analogously: "Culture is the sum total of human beings' collective efforts to come to grips symbolically with a complex and uncertain world." Lincoln, J. R. & Guillot, D. (2004). Durkheim and organizational culture. IRLE Working Paper No. 108-04, pp.4. Retrieved from http://irle.berkeley.edu/workingpapers/108-04.pdf

5 Although culture can and must be "built" it is also fundamentally dissipative. That is, while culture is derived from the shared mental models of people, those same people may leave the system and newcomers may enter it while the essential culture is maintained. See: Here We Jo. (2015, October 15). Brain games - social conformity [Video file]. Retrieved from https://www.youtube.com/watch?v=AegLdB7UI4U

6 Bruce Tharp, in a Haworth report, explains: "The culture of an organization eminently influences its myriad decisions and actions. A company's prevailing ideas, values, attitudes, and beliefs guide the way in which its employees think, feel, and act—quite often unconsciously." See: Tharp, B. (2009). Defining "culture" and "organizational culture": From anthropology to the office. Retrieved from http://www.thercfgroup.com/files/resources/Defining-Culture-and-Organizationa-Culture_5.pdf

7 Murray, A. (2016, March 3). The pinnacles and pitfalls of corporate culture. *Fortune.* Retrieved from http://fortune.com/2016/03/03/best-companies-to-work-for-editors-desk/

8 Taylor, S. (2013, July 21). The power of purpose: Why is a sense of purpose so essential for our well-being? *Psychology Today.* Retrieved from https://www.psychologytoday.com/blog/out-the-darkness/201307/the-power-purpose

9 Katzenbach, J., & Aguirre, D. (2013, May 28). Culture and the chief executive: CEOs are stepping up to a new role, as leaders of their company's thinking and behavior. *Strategy + Business.* Retrieved from https://www.strategy-business.com/article/00179?gko=6912e

10 While norms and values can be quite different—norms convey behavioral expectations that are often followed for varying reasons (including social pressure), whereas values are internalized beliefs that tend to be more enduring—it is important to recognize that they are both, fundamentally, mental models. This understanding helps elucidate the idea that culture is born of shared mental models that must be taught and inculcated among the group.

11 Lynch, M. (n.d.). Does anyone know where we keep the unwritten rules? [Cartoon]. Retrieved from from https://www.cartoonstock.com/directory/o/office_rules.asp

12 Lencioni, P. M. (2002). Make your values mean something. *Harvard Business Review, July.* Retrieved from https://hbr.org/2002/07/make-your-values-mean-something.

13 Hsieh, T. (2013). *Delivering happiness: a path to profits, passion, and purpose.* New York: Grand Central Publications.

14 Sandberg, S. (2013). *Lean in: women, work, and the will to lead.* New York: Knopf Doubleday Publishing Group.

15 Schultz, H. (2012). *Pour your heart into it: how Starbucks built a company one cup at a time.* New York, NY: Hachette Books.

16 Hsieh, T. (2013). *Delivering happiness: a path to profits, passion, and purpose.* New York: Grand Central Publications.

17 Stevens, M. (1994, October 3). I don't know how it started, either. All I know is that it's part of our corporate culture [Cartoon]. *The New Yorker.* Retrieved from http://www.mickstevens.com/

18 Cancialosi, C. (2015, March 2). 4 questions that will define a lasting corporate culture. *Forbes.* Retrieved from https://www.forbes.com/sites/chriscancialosi/2015/03/02/4-questions-that-will-define-a-lasting-corporate-culture

19 Nohria, N., & and Beer, M. (2000). Cracking the code of change. *Harvard Business Review,* May-June. Retrieved from https://hbr.org/2000/05/cracking-the-code-of-change

20 Raynaud-Richard, P. (2014, October 28). Engineering culture: code ownership [Blog post]. *Facebook Code.* Retrieved from https://code.facebook.com/posts/263824650408138/engineering-culture-series-code-ownership/

21 Davis, B. (2015, November 2). 17 bullshit-free quotes about company culture from digital organisations [Blog post]. *Econsultancy*. Retrieved from https://econsultancy.com/blog/67118-17-bullshit-free-quotes-about-company-culture-from-digital-organisations/

22 Goodson, S. (2012, March 25). How do you change your company's culture? Spark a movement. *Forbes*. Retrieved from https://www.forbes.com/sites/marketshare/2012/03/25/how-do-you-change-your-companys-culture-spark-a-movement/#459f95624e0c

23 Schultz, E. J. (2016). More marketers tasked with improving corporate culture. *Adage*. Retrieved from http://adage.com/article/print-edition/marketers-corporate-culture/302117/

24 The Clemmer Group. (2011, November 15). Is your culture by default or by design? [Blog post]. *The Clemmer Group*. Retrieved from https://www.clemmergroup.com/blog/2011/11/15/is-your-culture-by-default-or-by-design/

25 Berkun, S. (2014, April 21). A critique of "Don't fuck up the culture." [Blog post]. *Scott Berkun*. Retrieved from http://scottberkun.com/2014/critique-dont-fuck-up-culture/

26 Katzenbach, J., & Aguirre, D. (2013, May 28). Culture and the chief executive: CEOs are stepping up to a new role, as leaders of their company's thinking and behavior. *Strategy + Business*. Retrieved from https://www.strategy-business.com/article/00179?gko=6912e

27 First appeared as Management By Walking Around (MBWA) in Peters, T., & Waterman, R. (1982). *In search of excellence: Lessons from America's best-run companies*. New York: Harper & Row.

28 Peters, T., & Austin, N. (1985). *A passion for excellence: the leadership difference*. New York: Grand Central Publishing.

29 Chesky, B. (2014, April 20). Don't fuck up the culture. Medium [Blog]. Retrieved December 14, 2017, from https://medium.com/@bchesky/dont-fuck-up-the-culture-597cde9ee9d4#.nsaewkmug

30 Ewenstein, B., Smith, W., & Sologar, A. (2015). Changing change management. *McKinsey & Company*. Retrieved from http://www.mckinsey.com/global-themes/leadership/changing-change-management

31 Network dynamics, as always, are at play. Explaining why companies fail, Megan McArdle writes, "Even a dysfunctional culture, once well established, is astonishingly efficient at reproducing itself. The UCLA sociologist Gabriel Rossman told me, 'If new entrants assimilate to whatever is the majority at the time they enter, and if new entrants trickle in slowly, then the founding culture can persist over time, even if over the long run they make up a tiny minority.'" McArdle, M. (2012, March). Why companies fail. *The Atlantic, March 2012*. Retrieved from https://www.theatlantic.com/magazine/archive/2012/03/whycompanies-fail/308887/

32 Katzenbach, J., & Aguirre, D. (2013, May 28). Culture and the chief executive: CEOs are stepping up to a new role, as leaders of their company's thinking and behavior. *Strategy + Business*. Retrieved from https://www.strategy-business.com/article/00179?gko=6912e

33 Katzenbach, J., & Aguirre, D. (2013, May 28). Culture and the chief executive: CEOs are stepping up to a new role, as leaders of their company's thinking and behavior. *Strategy + Business*. Retrieved from https://www.strategy-business.com/article/00179?gko=6912e

34 Xie, J., Sreenivasan, S., Korniss, G., Zhang, W., Lim, C., & Szymanski, B. (2011). Social consensus through the influence of committed minorities. *Physical Review E, 84*(1). doi.org/10.1103/PhysRevE.84.011130

35 Oliver, P. (1993). Formal models of collective action. *Annu. Rev. Sociol, 19*, 271-300. doi.org/10.1146/annurev.so.19.080193.001415

36 Waldrop, M.M. (1996, October 10). Dee Hock on management. *Fast Company*. Retrieved from https://www.fastcompany.com/27454/dee-hock-management

37 The Clemmer Group. (2011, November 15). Is your culture by default or by design? [Blog post]. *The Clemmer Group*. Retrieved from https://www.clemmergroup.com/blog/2011/11/15/is-your-culture-by-default-or-by-design/

38 Katzenbach, J., & Aguirre, D. (2013, May 28). Culture and the chief executive: CEOs are stepping up to a new role, as leaders of their company's thinking and behavior. *Strategy + Business*. Retrieved from https://www.strategy-business.com/article/00179?gko=6912e

39 Collins, J. (2001). *Good to great: why some companies make the leap...... and others don't*. New York: HarperBusiness.

40 Proctor, P. (2014, May 14). A company really clicks when mission, brand and culture coverage. *Entrepreneur*. Retrieved from https://www.entrepreneur.com/article/233751#

41 Patel, S. (2015, August 6). 10 examples of companies with fantastic culture. *Entrepreneur*. Retrieved from https://www.entrepreneur.com/article/249174

42 Bock, L. (2015). *Work rules!: insights from inside Google that will transform how you live and lead*. New York, New York: Grand Central Publishing.